Lent Is Not Rocket Science:

An Exploration of God, Creation, and the Cosmos

Meditations for 40 Days of Lent

W. Nicholas Knisely

D1089635

Morehouse Publishing
NEW YORK · HARRISBURG · DENVER

Forward Movement
www.forwardmovement.org

Lent Is Not Rocket Science:

An Exploration of God, Creation, and the Cosmos

Meditations for 40 Days of Lent

Morehouse Publishing

New York • Harrisburg • Denver

Forward Movement

Cincinnati, Ohio

An Invitation to View Lent from a New Perspective

For a long time Christians understood that there were two ways to learn about God. One was by studying the revelations that God made through the writings collected into Holy Scripture. The other was by applying our senses to the world around, the creation that God made and then declared "very good" (Genesis 1:31) This second way of learning about God and God's intentions for humankind is called Natural Theology. The word theology literally means "words about God," so Natural Theology means "Nature's words about God."

During the Reformation in the sixteenth century, theologians began to become increasingly wary of humanity's ability to use reason properly. During the medieval period, the "scholastic" movement within theology had worked to apply the best of classical philosophical thought, primarily that of Aristotle, to reasoning about God. This way of thinking reasoned that the Earth was the center of the universe, that the lights in the sky revolved around it, and that planets moved because of the angels who propelled them with their wings. But as scientific observations about the nature of the solar system and gravity began to overthrow these ideas, theologians reacted by giving more importance to the revelation of Holy Scripture than that of Natural Theology. Today the situation has gotten so extreme in parts of the church that special courses taught in schools and universities focus on "Christian Science" and hold that anything that is seen to contradict the literal and plain meaning of Holy Scripture must be considered wrong and be dismissed. This leads some Christians to be suspicious of the study of evolution, cosmology, and geology.

During this Lent, I invite you to return to an earlier understanding of Natural Theology. I invite you to see it as a channel of revelation about the nature of God that is not absolute in itself, but is an equal partner in conversation with Holy Scriptures and the traditions of the church. Paying attention to the world around us—to the intricate structures of nature, to the mind-bending reality of the cosmic and microscopic realms—will invite us to recognize that the God we worship, and with whom we have an ongoing relationship, is present in the raging storm, the fiery whirlwind of the surface of a star, and the deep silence of intergalactic space.

I invite you to open all of your senses to seek God's presence in nature. God is not nature, nor is God bounded by nature, but God is most certainly nature's author—and nature's "words" can point us onward to that which is beyond its bounds. In the coming days and weeks of Lent, I invite you to journey from the largest scale of the created order inward to the very smallest scale we can speak about. Some of the images will be familiar, some of them will require a bit of meditation and imagination to understand, but all will hopefully lead us to new insights about God's relationship with us.

W. Nicholas Knisely
XIII Bishop of Rhode Island
Providence, Rhode Island
Lent 2014

Ash Wednesday

First the Fire

And the fire will test what sort of work each has done.

— 1 Corinthians 3:13

Many Episcopalians and other Christians will have ashes placed on their foreheads in the sign of the cross today. And many congregations make their ashes the day before, by burning the palms from the previous year's Palm Sunday service.

When I was a parish priest, I started asking people in the middle of the season of Epiphany to bring in any palms that had been blessed and that they wished to recycle. We collected the dried-out palms in a bag in the sacristy during the weeks leading up to Lent. After the traditional pancake supper on Fat Tuesday, the day of celebration before Ash Wednesday, I gathered the children to help me with burning the palms.

Over the years I had perfected my technique: Find an aluminum baking pan, a large tin can, and three small, similar-sized rocks. Place the rocks in the bottom of the pan. Use a can opener to take the top and bottom off the tin can so that it becomes a large empty cylinder. Place the cylinder on top of the three rocks. (Children and parents often asked me why I used three rocks, expecting that it had something to do with the Trinity or Richard Hooker's three-legged stool. I wish I had come up with a better explanation than the one that is the truth—it simply takes three points to make a stable balance for the cylinder.)

On Fat Tuesday I took the palms that we had collected and stuffed them down into the cylinder. I then used a long-necked butane lighter to light the palms on fire from the very bottom of the cylinder. As the bottoms of the palms smoldered, they gave off a growing cloud of tan smoke. Once the tan smoke was rising in a thick column, I put the long-necked lighter back down at the bottom of the can and made a new flame. That flame ignited the column of smoke into a column of fire, and the palms in the can rapidly turned to ash. (I always kept the children way back for this part, of course.) After the fire died out and the ashes were cooled, the children and I took forks and smashed the remaining ashes into smaller and smaller bits until only a fine powder remained. I used that fine powder the next day as the dust for Ash Wednesday.

The reason the second small flame makes such a dramatic change is because when something "burns" what actually ignites are the gasses given off by the material that is decomposing in the heat. The gas is the release of all the complicated organic molecules that the palm tree gathered from the soil and the atmosphere, then combined with the rainwater from the sky and the energy of the sunlight, and stored in the cells of its branches. The first fire that I lit started taking apart all that work, so that the organic molecules trapped in the cellulose of the palm would be freed and lit. The second flame ignited the gasses in the rising column of tan smoke, and their ignition created the small fireball and dramatic column of flame.

I find it very evocative that the ashes we use on this day come from the destruction of the work of creation. The microbes and cellular creatures of creation labored for years to organize the minerals and chemicals that made up the structure of the leaf of palm. When we cut the leaf off the tree, taking it away from its source of nourishment and water, those cells began to die. They dried out and become mere husks of what they once were. But the fire of Fat Tuesday released the molecules back into the atmosphere so that a new plant could use them again. Fire, water, air, and Earth are all present in the moment of the creation of the ashes. And though we put the end product on our foreheads, the life-giving parts have been returned to creation to be used again and again.

In our own lives there are times when the fire must come to release the elements we've stored up in careful, complicated containers in our hearts. Ash Wednesday reminds us not to fear that experience but to see in it the wonder of God's economy, the working out of the plan of creation and salvation.

❧

Where is the fire going to come into your heart this Lent?

And what will it release to others?

What needs to be broken down in you to release the fire of the Holy Spirit in your life this Lent?

Thursday after Ash Wednesday

Joseph Butler and the *Analogy*

My beloved speaks and says to me:
"Arise, my love, my fair one, and come away."

— The Song of Solomon 2:10

How should science and religion speak to each other? It's not clear. Science is built on a ladder of deductions and observations. Religion, particularly in the case of Christianity, is built on revelation and experience. Given that the two disciplines are different at this fundamental level, finding a common language has always been difficult.

In the earliest days of the church, there was no divide between natural philosophy and theology. One led directly to the other, and people studied natural philosophy—what we typically call "science" today—on the way to their work in theology. But during the Renaissance of Western thought, when pre-Christian thinkers were being rediscovered and studied, a gulf began to grow between the two disciplines. The way scientists and theologians did their work became an increasing barrier to the conversation many expected them to have. The problem became more acute as time went by.

Joseph Butler, Bishop of Durham in the mid-eighteenth century, wrote a book that was primarily a response to the new thinking that Isaac Newton's work had begun. Newton's laws of motion and gravitation allowed the natural philosophers of his day to make predictions that were a revelation to their time. Things we take for granted today—like predicting the exact date of an eclipse, describing the flight of a canon ball, or understanding how a barrel of water drains from a spigot—became commonplace for the first time as a result of Newton's work. The universe was no longer viewed as a living entity with the Holy Spirit as its core, but as a machine, a mechanism that was understandable and predictable. A new view of God began to emerge—the clock-maker God who, having set the universe in motion, had left the scene and was no longer in constant relationship with it.

Butler's work, titled *Analogy of Religion Natural and Revealed to the Constitution and Course of Nature* but commonly known as the *Analogy,* was considered a tour de force in his day. He undertook to show how the best scientific thinking of his day was not opposed at all to the theology of the church. Rather, he said, all of nature pointed toward the deeper revelation of God. He began by describing the butterfly that emerges from the cocoon transformed with a new and more glorious body as an analogy of what God intended for each of us—and the whole of creation—in the coming kingdom. Butler's work became the talk of northern Europe, and for a while it was one of the most popular books in print.

But then scientific thought moved on. The French and German schools began to move beyond Newton's mechanical models for the universe and toward a view based on the behavior of energy in all its various forms. Butler's book was now having a conversation with a partner that was no longer speaking with it. Christianity, based on the full revelation of God in the person of Jesus, speaks of eternal truths that must be at the heart of all theological conversations no matter the era in which they occur. Science, however, is constantly moving forward, discarding older ideas that are no longer viewed as adequate explanations and taking up new ones that promise to do a better job of explaining what is observed. It's not that the two conversation partners have a different language; they are each speaking in ways to which the other has trouble relating.

And yet we need to have the conversation. And so we struggle to hear each other's voice. There can be no reconciliation, which is the core of the church's mission, unless there is conversation. It has always seemed to me that learning to speak to each other, learning to understand how another person thinks, is both the key to empathy and compassion but also a primary gate to be entered as we come into the kingdom of God.

⥁

What conversations have you been neglecting because they are difficult to have?

Who in your life do you have trouble identifying with or understanding?

What can you do today to move a little closer to those persons, to take the conversation a few steps further along? Doing that is doing the work of reconciliation.

Friday after Ash Wednesday

Don't Make the Bible a Liar

Lead me in your truth, and teach me.

— Psalm 25:4

Most of the perceived conflict between science and religion is rooted in how we understand the role of the Bible in the church. For most of the church's history, the Bible was understood to be authoritative for Christians and worthy to be studied by all. But it was used as a conversation partner and not as a rule book.

This is seen very clearly in some of the writings of Saint Augustine of Hippo. Augustine's understanding of how we are justified by our faith and not by our works came from his deep study of Saint Paul's writings. But when it came to defending biblical accounts of creation against criticisms made by pagan philosophers, Augustine argued that it was a mistake to insist on the biblical account as literal truth in all instances. To people who insisted that natural laws didn't apply, Augustine responded: "It is disgrace for a Christian to talk nonsense to a pagan about something the pagan knows about—because it causes them to doubt everything that is found in the books of the Bible." (He was specifically referencing the movement and relative sizes of the heavenly bodies.)

Augustine's point is that we when try to use the Bible's witness incorrectly, we damage the Bible's witness to the primary matters to which it testifies: the story of God's relationship with Israel, the coming of the Messiah, and the death and resurrection of Jesus. The way the books of the Bible were misused in Augustine's day is still happening in ours. The current misuse is a reaction to the ascendency of the scientific method, specifically Darwin's work in natural selection as the origin of the diversity of life. There's a sense in some parts of the church that we can read the Bible the way we read a textbook, and that every single verse of the Bible has an eternal truth to teach. There's a differing model in other parts of the church that says the stories contained in the text—and, of course, the metastory that the entire library of books tells as a whole—are the most important. There's no one single model on how to read and understand the Bible, and that's the root cause of much of the conflict within the church today.

So this Lent, as we begin to think about how the natural world testifies to the hand of God in creation, it's important for us to take some time to think about how we each understand the Bible.

How do you understand the Bible?

Have you thought much about it?

Do you think all the various parts of the Bible are equally true?

Are there different kinds of truth?

Episcopal clergy testify at their ordination that they believe the Bible is the Word of God and contains all things necessary to salvation. What do you think that means?

Saturday after Ash Wednesday

The Limits of Logic

You will know the truth,
and the truth will make you free.

— John 8:32

One of the great mistakes people make is to believe that things that are true can be shown to be true by the use of deductive reasoning and logic. I think the roots of this belief come from the way we are educated as children, when we learn facts in a systematic way and arrange truths in a logical order. You can see this most clearly in the way we learn mathematics, particularly as students move from elementary school classes in arithmetic into junior high and high school courses in algebra and geometry. Teachers start with the basic axioms, things that we accept as true without needing proofs. We use those axioms to prove more complicated ideas, and then use those proofs to support more and more sophisticated conjectures.

The student is left with the idea that mathematics is a beautiful, organized ladder that starts with simple things and climbs up by use of logic and deduction to ever more complicated ideas.

The same idea underlies much of the physical sciences, given that they are, to the greatest extent possible, driven by theories that are logically derived and experimentally verified. Certainly the great triumphs of Kepler, Galileo, and Newton in mechanics and celestial movements start with the very simplest laws possible and then extend them to explain and accurately predict the intricate movements of the world.

A rather famous mathematician named Kurt Gödel threw a huge monkey wrench into the whole logical enterprise when he rigorously proved that there were things that were true that could not be proven true using logical deduction. (It's a bit more sophisticated than that, but basically that's his idea.) Gödel's incompleteness theorem means that logic won't get us to all truth. In fact it says that we can't even hope that it will get us to most truth. Logic is a powerful but limited tool. At least when we look at logic logically.

Many people of faith worry about not being able to logically prove or experimentally verify their beliefs. And there are certainly voices in the world around us for whom this inability is seen as a fatal flaw in the religious enterprise. But if we hold Gödel's idea before us, we can understand that this lack of logic isn't a fatal flaw; it just indicates that religious truth has to be handled with a different set of tools. The big question for us is to discover what those tools might be.

While you're pondering that, you might reflect on the spiritual significance of limitations. Logic is limited in its utility. God limits God's self in the act of Incarnation. You and I are taking on the spiritual discipline of limitations in the season of Lent. Sometimes the decision to limit our choices makes space for creativity to flourish and allows new ideas to emerge.

✎

How do we know if a religious idea is true?

Is it because it's logically proven from the Bible?

Is it because the church has found it useful over time?

Is it because it makes you a better, more loving person?

How do we know our faith is true?

First Sunday in Lent

Cosmos

O Lord and Ruler of the hosts of heaven...
You made the heavens and the earth,
with all their vast array.

— *The Book of Common Prayer,* Canticle 14, p. 90

In this first week of Lent, I invite you to meditate with me on the largest structures of God's creation. Not the large things that we on Earth have seen or created, but structures that fill the sky and are fundamental to the organization of the universe and our own existence. I invite you to meditate with me on what we can learn by looking at the darkness of the night sky, the sameness of creation over vast distances, the meaning of time, and more.

On this first Sunday in Lent, as many of us begin our yearly pilgrimage in a formal way, I ask you to consider the scale of creation. Much of what I will present over the next weeks is organized by scale, beginning at the largest, the cosmic scale, and ending in the last days of Lent and Holy Week at the smallest, the quantum scales. The greatest conundrum in my mind is that it is possible for us to use our imagination to conceive the cosmos.

The universe is essentially a giant empty, soundless, cold, chaotic void. In incredibly rare instances, there are small pockets of organized matter. The little pockets represent very simple things like electrons, a proton, a cosmic ray. Even more rarely those little bits of organization combine into something complicated—a hydrogen or helium atom. Even more rare than that are clouds of hydrogen. Stars, planets, and everything else that we can see are very small and very rare things when we think on the cosmic scale. It's hard to imagine that God fills all of this vastness with the fire of love, or that God can comprehend its totality.

And yet that is just what we insist on believing about God as Christians. And more than that, we believe that the same God who animates the vast cosmos knows each of us individually by name and loves us. And that God came into the cosmos at a specific moment in history here on the Earth, a nondescript rocky planet in orbit around a boringly typical and relatively small star.

It is when I think about the universe at the largest cosmic scales that I am most dumbfounded by what theologians call the "scandal of the particularity of the Incarnation." We are so small and yet for some reason we matter so much to God. It is a thing nearly impossible to grasp. And yet it is central to the teaching of the prophets and the apostles.

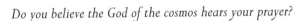

Do you believe the God of the cosmos hears your prayer?

If you find yourself struggling with that, could you, at least for today, envision what would change in you if you believed that?

Monday,
First Week in Lent

Olbers' Paradox

The heavens declare the glory of God,
and the firmament shows his handiwork.

— Psalm 19:1

There are a number of jokes that start with a child asking an adult, "Why is the sky blue?" But to the best of my memory, I've never heard any child ask, "Why is the sky dark at night?" Both questions turn out to have very interesting answers, but the latter question has much deeper implications.

The answer to the question about the dark sky at night requires us to think a bit about what we know of the universe. Prior to the last century, scientists of the Enlightenment believed the universe had always existed and was of infinite extent. But that infinity of scale creates a problem when we think about our dark night sky. Imagine you are standing deep in the woods of a forest. The foliage and the undergrowth are so thick that no matter what direction you look, you see a green leaf. In the deepest parts of the forest, or in a fully grown rain forest, it is impossible to see the horizon or sometimes even the sky. The forest floor is kept in a perpetual twilight even in the middle of the day, because wherever you are standing, eventually there's a plant with a leaf blocking your view of the blue sky.

Now imagine you're standing in the middle of the desert looking up into the night sky. You see that the sky is filled with stars, each one a small point of light. In part of the sky, when we look out into the plane of our own galaxy, the stars appear so close together that it looks like there is a glowing cloud that stretches all the way around the sky. That cloud of light appears because as we look into the heart of our Milky Way Galaxy, our line of sight eventually finds a star that blocks it from looking further.

If the universe is of infinite extent, then it stands to reason that no matter where we look in the sky, we will eventually see a star. The star may be very, very far away and we may see only a tiny,

tiny bit of its light, but if you multiply even a tiny number by infinity, you still get infinity. So, no matter how little light we see from one star, the total amount of light that we see should be very, very bright—as if we were looking directly at the surface of the sun at noontime.

The fact that we see a darkened sky at night when logically we shouldn't is called Olbers' Paradox. A number of scientists and philosophers have tried to work out a resolution to this contradiction from the time Heinrich Olbers first proposed it. Interestingly enough, the writer Edgar Allan Poe first pointed the way to resolving the paradox. He suggested that the only way to understand what we see in the darkness of the night was to conclude that the universe was not infinite. It either had an edge—something scientists didn't want to accept—or it must have had a beginning. If it had a beginning, then even if the universe is infinite, we couldn't see all of it. We could only see the portion that is as far away as light has traveled since the moment of the universe's beginning—its "Genesis."

Isn't it extraordinary to be able to go outside at night and look up into the dark night sky and realize that the sky is dark because the universe had a beginning? The simple experience of nighttime proves to us that time had a start and that the universe has a history. Then it's not too far a line of reason to start to wonder why the beginning happened, and what or who caused it.

The dark sky invites us to wonder about the existence of the Creator.

Paying attention to the smallest things in our day-to-day existence can take us into the presence of the greatest questions and answers of human experience.

Today, pay attention to what you experience and take on the spiritual discipline of asking yourself, "Why?"

Tuesday, First Week in Lent

Uniform Temperature

In the beginning...

— Genesis 1:1

If you put two pots of water in a room and take their temperature immediately afterwards, they will not be at the same exact temperature. Even if you fill them from the same faucet, the water will warm or chill over the time the faucet is open, because the first bit of water that was flowing was stored in the pipes in the walls and the next bit is being drawn from pipes underground. If the two pots of water had exactly the same temperature, then you'd have to either be surprised at something that is extremely unlikely or try to work out in your head how this surprising result came to be.

The simplest explanation would be that the water in the two pots came from a third pot that held the waters together long enough that they came to equilibrium with each other. Or perhaps the two pots were touching each other as they were filled, and they were able to exchange their heat or chill through the walls of the pots in the time that they were in contact with each other. In either case, the water in the one pot must have somehow been "told" the temperature of the other pot so that the two could come to be the same temperature.

One of the most extraordinary surprises in the early 1960s, when scientists measured the temperature of the deep space by pointing microwave "thermometers" toward the stars, was that the sky turned out to be not absolutely cold. This information wasn't a huge surprise, given that some scientists had been convinced the universe had begun in a gigantic fiery explosion of light. But the surprise was that no matter what direction you looked, the temperature was, for all intents and purposes, the same. Remembering the question of the temperature of the two pots of water, how did it come to be that one side of the sky was able to "know" the temperature of the other side? Even if they had sent a message to each other at the speed of light, we are in the middle of them and their two messages are just now at the halfway point.

The answer turned out to be that the universe, which began in the fiery explosion, was very, very small initially. Even though the part of the universe on one side of the sky is too far away to have "talked" to the other side of the sky, the two sides of the sky were once in the same exact place. So while they are rushing apart from each other in the universe's expansion, they "remember" the information they knew in the beginning of creation.

That turns out to be true for everything in the universe, because everything in the universe was once one. Every particle of matter that is contained in your body and mine were once one. Every particle of matter that is found on the Earth was once one. Every ghostly subatomic particle that is hurtling through the outer darkness of the universe was once part of all of us. In the moment of creation, we were once one. And there are certain properties that we all share because of that moment of unity.

I find this to be more than just a beautiful poetic image. The reality that every part of the universe "knew" and "experienced" every other part of the universe is what makes much of scientific thought possible today. We can assert that the physics that works here on Earth works the same way in another region of the universe because every electron shares the same charge, and every proton the same mass, etc. And they do that because they were calibrated together in the moment of creation.

We Christians believe that God created us all. We believe that it was God who was the prime cause of the beginning. And that while God is more than the light and fire of the beginning of creation, God was present in it. If God was present in that, then God is present in us and the whole of the universe, just as we are present to the whole of the universe and to God.

When you look into the deep darkness of the nighttime sky, you are seeing matter and energy that is fundamentally connected with you. When Saint Francis talked about the elements of creation as our sister or our brother, he was much more right than anyone ever suspected.

～

What will you do today to celebrate this extraordinary family of which you are an equal member?

Wednesday,
First Week in Lent

Looking Back into Time

Your Father knows what you need before you ask him.

— Matthew 6:8

Light travels very fast. But its speed, while fast in human terms, is still finite. So when we look out from the Earth's surface toward things in the sky, beyond the Earth's atmosphere, we are seeing things as they *were*, not as they are.

Light takes a few seconds to travel to the Earth from the moon, its closest planetary object. Light takes about eight minutes to travel from the sun. The outer planets of the solar system represent a distance of an hour of light's travel time. We can talk about distances to celestial objects in terms of millions of miles, but the numbers get so large so quickly that we tend to talk about distance in terms of the time it takes for light to get to us from the object. A light year is the distance that light travels in one year. It's many, many trillions of miles.

The closest stars to us are four to ten light years away. The center of our galaxy is about 25,000 light years away. The Milky Way is about 100,000 light years in diameter. And the Andromeda Galaxy (the closest large galaxy to ours) is about 2,500,000 light years away. The distances become unimaginable as we move further out into the universe.

But this also means that we are seeing nothing in the sky as it actually is at the moment. We see the sun as it was about eight minutes ago. We see the stars in the Milky Way Galaxy as they were hundreds or thousands of years ago. And we see the other galaxies as they were millions or billions of years ago. The further out we look from the Earth, the further back into history we are seeing and the less we know about the present situation. Astronomers call this "look back time," and it's both a challenge and a tool for doing scientific research.

It seems to me that the same phenomenon is present in our human relationships. What we know of people, especially those not present in our lives in an active way, is what we knew of them when we last saw them, not as they are now. I remember how someone behaved when he or she was a regular part of my life and think that I know the person.

But people change, sometimes rapidly and occasionally radically. When I think about people, and pray for them and their needs, I have to remember that I don't generally know them as they are now, so I don't know who they are or what they really need. I try to remember that I am praying to God for God to do what is needed in that moment—not what I think they need based on my outdated ideas.

It's rather striking that the one person we are in relationship with at all times, who knows what we need in any given moment, is God. I may not know what the rest of the universe actually looks like now, and I may not know what my friends, enemies, and loved ones need right now, but God does. Our ongoing relationships with God create the bonds of love that knit all the instants of reality together. God is a simple way of looking at things this way, the root of our existence.

For whom are you praying today?

Are you praying for what they have asked for, or for what you believe they need?

How often do you pray for yourself?

Thursday, First Week in Lent

Dark Matter

No eye has seen, nor ear heard,
nor the human heart conceived,
what God has prepared.

— 1 Corinthians 2:9

Much of the work of physics in the past century was concerned with uncovering the basic building blocks of nature. Over a period of about 120 years, we have discovered the electron, the proton, and the neutron, and then learned that the proton and the neutron were made of up and down quarks. We've learned about photons and $W\pm$ particles, muons and neutrinos, and many more exotic particles. No one is really convinced that we have discovered all the pieces that make up the universe, but until recently, we thought we knew where we ought to be looking.

Odd behavior in the ways that galaxies rotate caused astronomers to begin to look for some sort of matter that appeared to be changing the gravitation around galaxies but couldn't be detected in the normal sorts of ways. They called this "dark matter," because there was no light associated with it at all. And people began to try to understand how much of the universe was made up of this mysterious stuff.

After looking at the large-scale behavior of the universe, some odd features about the way the Big Bang explosion evolved, and other disconnected pieces of evidence, most astronomers and physicists are convinced that the normal everyday matter that the stars, the galaxies, and we are made of represents at best 10 percent of the matter in the universe. The other 90 percent, the large bulk of all the material of creation, is invisible to us. It's not just invisible—it's so mysterious we have no idea what it is. Most models tell us it's something that causes gravity, but other than that, it's unlike any other matter. We don't know what it is, and we don't know where to look.

It surrounds us, it's not predicted by any major theory, and it appears as yet to be unobservable. And it's nine times more common than everything we can see lit up in the sky.

Whenever anyone tells you that there's no scientific basis for believing in matters of faith or in miracles, you might remember that there's no scientific basis for our discovering that the stuff we are made of is just a small part of a mysterious whole. Who knows what it is that surrounds us in every direction, has given rise to the galaxies, caused the stars to form in their unique ways, and essentially modified all of reality? It's not right to call it "god stuff," but its existence is a reminder that there are plenty of shortcomings and unexplained things in science. No one knows what it all will turn out to be. To say that science leaves no room for mystery would be a terrible mistake.

❧

Where is mystery for you today?

What is unexplainable, unexpected, and too striking to be just a coincidence?

Where is God or the divine found in the mystery today?

Is the mystery that you encounter this day big enough or wide enough that you are forced to admit how little you know, even though we've become very successful at explaining things?

Friday,
First Week in Lent

Where Is the Center?

You are precious in my sight, and honored,
and I love you.

— Isaiah 43:4

One of the basic axioms of Einstein's relativity theory is the assertion that there is no "privileged" reference frame. What he meant was that physics must be the same for everyone, and to make that happen, at least mathematically, you have to insist that all observers have the right to claim they are "at rest" no matter where they are, as long as they are moving with a constant velocity.

The easiest way to understand this is to think about what it's like to ride in a car driving at a constant speed down the highway. Inside the car, everything behaves as if the car were standing still. The coffee in your cup stays level in your cup. If you drop something, it falls straight down inside the car. But if you are accelerating, or going around a curve, you know that the coffee in the cup might slosh out, and when you drop something, it falls at an unexpected angle. As long as you move at the same speed, everything behaves like it does when you're parked in your driveway. If your windows were painted black and you couldn't see out them, you would be able to claim that you were parked in your own driveway—and, other than the engine noise and the bumps in the road, it would be hard to prove you wrong.

As Einstein formulates this principle in a more rigorous way, there's a surprising consequence: each one of us can claim to be the center of the universe. And it's impossible to prove that claim wrong. We can claim that the Earth is the center of the universe, we can claim that the sun is the center of the universe, we can claim that the Milky Way Galaxy is the center of the universe, we can claim that any galaxy or star or planet is the center, and there's no way to disprove that claim.

We are all the center of the universe and none of us is the center of the universe—at least as far as Einstein is concerned.

It's not too hard to see a spiritual corollary to this idea is it? Because of God's love for us as individuals, we are each at the center of the purpose of creation. But because of God's infinite love for the rest of creation, everyone else is also, individually, at the center of the purpose of creation. We are each infinitely important and infinitesimally important to God. We have every right to be righteous with pride and every reason to be profoundly humble when we encounter another human being.

～

Can you practice a spiritual discipline today of seeing yourself as the center of creation?

Can you spend the day seeing each person you are with, one at a time, as the center of God's creation? Which of the two ways of seeing is easier?

Why?

Saturday,
First Week in Lent

The Copernican Principle

You yourself created my inmost parts;
you knit me together in my mother's womb.
I will thank you because I am marvelously made;
your works are wonderful, and I know it well.

— Psalm 139:12-13

Most of us know of Nicolaus Copernicus, the Polish astronomer and clergy person, as the man who showed that the sun was at the center of the universe and the Earth revolved around it. But that's both oversimplifying his work and understating what he did. In his posthumously published book, he essentially writes that he's not actually claiming the sun is at the center of the universe, but just that he's found an excellent mathematical device to make the calculation of planetary motion (as seen from the Earth) easier.

But the relatively weak claim may have been the result of his intuitive understanding that what he was really doing was overturning the intellectual ordering of the entire universe: scientifically, philosophically, and theologically. Copernicus seemed to understand that this revolution in thought was going to be resisted and at least initially rejected. And he was right, even though no one understood the full implications for centuries.

By moving the Earth away from the "center" of the universe, Copernicus was essentially demoting humanity as well. We were no longer "special" or in a "special place" in creation. We were on the third rock from the sun. There were other planets closer and more planets farther away. It meant that the sun, the moon, and all the other planets did not revolve around us; we all revolved around the sun. We were not privileged observers of the universe.

This idea that we are not special, that what we experience and observe must be typical for any person in the universe, turns out to be an incredibly powerful tool for scientific work. If we are special, we cannot assume that the physical laws which are true here on Earth would be the same for a planet around another star, or that what is true now was true in the past and will be true in the future of the universe. This Copernican principle is at the heart of most astronomy and cosmology. If we are special, then we can't extend our observations about our experience and make deductions about the rest of creation.

Take a moment and think about that today. Because it seems to me that the Copernican principle and a sort of corresponding social egalitarianism is at the heart of the second half of Jesus' summary of the law: "You shall love your neighbor as yourself." If you are not special, then neither is your neighbor. You are both beloved children of God. Your experience of being human is not unique to you. Your sense of worth and your sense of value must be true for others as well.

Do you believe this?

Do you live it?

Second Sunday in Lent

The Stars

What is man that you should be mindful of him?

— Psalm 8:5

In this second week of Lent, we are going to change our perspective from asking questions of the whole of the universe and instead look at just the galaxy, our island universe. The Milky Way Galaxy, where the sun is presently found in one of the spiral arms while it is orbiting the central black hole, is about 100,000 light years in diameter. We make a complete revolution around the galaxy about once every quarter of a billion years; so using the commonly accepted age of the Earth as about five billion years, we've toured around the whole of the galaxy about twenty times.

The distances and the timescale of the galaxy and vast reaches of empty space between the stars are hard for us to imagine. But the galaxy seems relatively cozy compared with the near absolute emptiness of the spaces between the galaxies.

But even that space, which, in terms of galactic scales, is not terribly large (maybe a few dozen galactic radii at most) is dwarfed by the great voids of empty space that make up the reaches of the universe between the clustered and super-clustered neighborhoods where the galaxies are found.

Yet God is in all of this. God is found in the whirling energy at the core of the galaxy and God is found in the hot stellar nurseries where new stars are being born. God is found in tombstones of dead stars, the spinning neutron star pulsars that keep inhumanly imaginable perfect time and serve as galactic navigation beacons. And God is found in vast, cold, empty space—the majority of our universe—where there will never be sound or light.

Trying to imagine God filling all the vast array of interstellar and intergalactic space causes me to stop and wonder that the same God is mindful of humanity. It is beyond my—or probably anyone's—ability to comprehend. And yet it is what God tells us, what Jesus insists on when he says that God knows our daily needs and even the number of the hairs on our head. How this can be, and what it means then to be human, are frequent sources of wonder for me in my prayer life.

This week, as we turn to the galaxy and the stars, keep in mind that God is found in the midst of this grand scale of creation. Look for God in the small things in your life this week as you contemplate the God of the galaxies as well.

Is it possible for you to see God's constant action in history?

What will you pray for God to do next in history?

Where do you see God in the daily news today?

Where do you see God in the small things in your life?

Monday,
Second Week in Lent

Stellar Equilibrium

Lord, you have searched me out and known me;
you know my sitting down and my rising up.

— Psalm 139:1

When we look upon a star, what we are actually seeing is a delicate balance between massive forces that are simultaneously working to explode the star and collapse it.

Stars are essentially gigantic clouds of elemental gas, primarily hydrogen, that are organized by gravitational attraction into a roughly spherical shape. The core of the star is unimaginably hot, and the atmosphere cools (relatively speaking) as you move out from the center toward the "light sphere" of the star. What we see as the "surface" of the gaseous star is actually the coolest region. The stellar atmosphere begins to heat again as you continue to move out from the surface.

The heat in the core of the star and the incredible density of the gas crushed together by the gravitational attraction of all that material allows a sustained thermonuclear reaction to take place. This nuclear furnace heats the core matter and pushes it outward. This outward pressure is exactly balanced by the gravitational pressure that pushes the same matter inward in an attempt to collapse the gas further and make it even more dense.

If the star manages to push back more strongly than its own gravity, the gas has more room and starts to cool, which reduces the outward pressure of expansion and allows gravity to squeeze the star back to its original size. If gravity's outward pressure begins to dominate, the collapsing gas heats up and creates more outward pressure, which pushes against the gravitational force and causes the star to expand. The balance of these two forces allows the star to find a stable existence that lasts, in some cases, for billions and billions of years. In principle, there are stars that are so stable they have lifetimes nearly the same as the universe.

This extraordinary balance between opposing forces creates the stability that allows stars to shine as beacons across the arms of our galaxy. It seems to me that there are similar balancing forces in society and in our own lives that, if we cooperate with the balancing, allow similar sorts of long-term stability. In some ways, The Episcopal Church is an excellent example of this balancing act, because it embraces the "Elizabethan Settlement"—the idea that we can say words in common, but not insist that we understand their meaning in the same way.

When you look upon a star, try not to see only the fantastic light that is shining across time and space. Try also to see it as a reminder that we have to find a healthy balance in our physical and spiritual lives.

What are the forces in your life that balance you and allow you to find stability?

How much do you need to participate in that balance?

How much attention are you paying to it right now?

Where is God in this balance?

Tuesday,
Second Week in Lent

Selection Effect in the
Hertzsprung-Russell Diagram

For now we see in a mirror, dimly.

— 1 Corinthians 13:12

When you look out into the dark sky at night, the twinkling stars lead you to believe something about the universe that isn't accurate.

It's hard to tell what color a star is when looking at it in the dark. The parts of our eye that let us see things in dim light evolved to see shape and movement, but not color. That makes sense in a dark forest filled with predators, but it is a bit of a bother when you are trying to tell whether a star is red or yellow or green or blue. A few stars are obviously red—some are often mistaken for the planet Mars. But to most of us, the stars look whitish blue when viewed with the naked eye.

If you use a telescope or a spectrograph, the colors of the star are more apparent and even measurable. Scientists like things that are measurable, and when astronomers are trying to find patterns that might lead to a new understanding, they often use a graph to plot what they are measuring. A particularly useful way of plotting the colors of the stars and their brightness is called a Hertzsprung-Russell diagram.

If you plot the stars that can be seen with the naked eye from Earth, you'll notice that most of the data clusters toward the blue and very bright region of the graph. And if you plot the data we know about the stars that are closest to the Earth (not just the ones we see with the naked eye), you'll see the stars cluster on the opposite region of the graph—in the redder, dimmer region. The difference between the two graphs is very striking. The stars we see and stars that are closest to us are very different in character.

That's not terribly surprising if you think about it. The brighter a star is, the further away it can be seen. Some of the brightest naked-eye stars in the sky are enormous blue-white giants that turn out to be very, very far away from us. The dim red stars are very numerous but can't be seen by our eye except in our own interstellar neighborhood. The fact that we see the enormous galactic lighthouse stars with our eyes, and the dimmer red stars only with special instruments, has led us to imagine that all stars are white.

Human beings can often be misled by what they see with their own two eyes. We think we are seeing the whole picture, when in fact we are only seeing what we are able to perceive. It's only with careful, systematic observation that we can pull aside the veil, as it were, and see the reality of what is happening. That's true with the night sky, and I think it's true for us spiritually as well.

That's the real challenge. We need to learn to see in a patient way, not leaping to generalize our experience and attempting, willy-nilly, to use our experience to understand others. I imagine some of the confusion we see in the gospels and the epistles about the acts and teachings of Jesus stems from this habit. We know something of God, but when confronted with the full truth of God, we realize that we know only in part.

≈

What can you do today to see patiently and methodically instead of leaping to a conclusion about something new you encounter?

Wednesday, Second Week in Lent

The Bigger They Are, the Faster They Disappear

Now there was a great wind...
but the LORD was not in the wind;
and after the wind an earthquake,
but the LORD was not in the earthquake;
and after the earthquake a fire,
but the LORD was not in the fire;
and after the fire a sound of sheer silence.

— 1 Kings 19:11-12

When I was a freshman in college taking an introductory astronomy class, my professor talked about the giant blue stars that are essentially the lighthouses of the galaxy as being the party stars of the universe. He meant that they were born fast, lived hard, and died young. At least in stellar terms.

The bigger a cloud of hydrogen gas is, the more mass it contains. And the more mass, the stronger the gravitational attraction. And the stronger the attraction, the more quickly the cloud of gas collapses, heats up, and starts to "burn" with nuclear fire. And in a sort of paraphrase of the words of Jesus, to those stars who have much, more will be given, because the larger mass and stronger gravity have the effect of making the nuclear fire at the core of the star much more efficient than what you'd see in a smaller, less massive star. So the big blue stars burn fast and burn hot. And because they burn so well, they quickly exhaust the fuel they have to burn. Very quickly, they start the final stages of a star's life cycle, and, depending on the size, either explode in a supernova or blow off most of their mass in a moment of rapid expansion caused by the flash of new nuclear fire at their core.

The little stars have a much different sort of life. The gas cloud from which they are formed takes a relatively long time to collapse. There's not much matter there, and if it moves or is stirred in any way, it takes longer for the core of the cloud to get to the critical density required for the nuclear reactions to begin and for the star to start to shine.

And because it's smaller and the pressure at the center is less, the fires are less "intense" and the star is cooler, redder. The red stars manage to sputter along for a very long time. Whereas a blue giant star might live a quarter of a billion years, a small red star has a lifespan easily in excess of the present age of the universe (about 14 billion years or so) and might be able to continue its life as a star for nearly 50 billion years or more.

The blue giant stars attract all the attention. They shine as brilliant beacons visible anywhere in the galaxy—and in some cases are visible to far distant galaxies. But they soon exhaust themselves. The red stars, the little stars, manage, in a quiet way, to keep on burning, lighting up their region of interstellar space for unimaginably long periods. The things that attract our attention are ephemeral and temporary. That which we barely notice is that which endures.

There's an obvious spiritual parallel here, I think. So much of what we notice in our lives are the things that grab our attention. But we soon either tire of them or they turn out to have no lasting power. The smaller, simpler things—

things we often take for granted—are the things that endure. The little things, the quiet things, are most often the places where we encounter the stability that allows us to more fully see the purpose of creation.

❧

What in your life is commanding your attention right now?

Is it something that will last? Or is it a desire or idea that, though it burns bright, will soon disappear?

And what is there in your life right now that you might miss if you didn't pay attention—that will endure and give life in the long term?

Where will you choose to focus your attention today?

Thursday,
Second Week in Lent

Exo-planets and How Unique We Are

Lift up your eyes on high and see: Who created these?
He who brings out their host and numbers them,
calling them all by name;
because he is great in strength, mighty in power,
not one is missing.

— Isaiah 40:26

Are there other civilizations like ours in the Milky Way Galaxy? Is someone out there that we could talk to? Is someone out there for us to visit, or who might visit us? These are some of the most fundamental questions humans have asked. And it's at the heart of much of the scientific study of the galaxy.

In 1961, Frank Drake, an American astronomer, tried to determine if there were other alien civilizations in our galaxy and, if so, how many. He started by trying to estimate how many stars were in the galaxy, and then what percentage of those stars had planets, and what percentage of those planets were "earth-like," and on and on. Some of the numbers, like how many stars there are in our galaxy, we know reasonably well. But questions like how many of those stars have planets, and how many of those planets are habitable, and how many of those planets may have life, and so on were complete and total guesses. At least until recently.

With new technology and new telescopes, astronomers have been able to start finding planets both orbiting stars and occasionally wandering by themselves through interstellar space. The first few discoveries were newsworthy, not just because they were very difficult observations to make, but also because the observations give us a better sense of the likelihood that other stars have planets orbiting them. But lately, the new discoveries of planets orbiting other stars have become almost routine, ignored in the press and popular media, unless there's something extraordinary about them, such as the planet's size or how close or far it is orbiting from its star.

It's beginning to look like many stars have planets. But it's also beginning to look like very

Forty Days of Lent

few stars have planets strung out the way our sun has them, and even fewer appear to have rocky planets in what is called the "life zone"—the region around a star where the planet's surface temperature allows liquid water to collect on its surface. (Liquid water is thought to be a key feature that allows for the existence of the kinds of complex organic molecules that are vital to making even the simplest forms of terrestrial life possible.)

If this continues to be the case, as we continue to refine our ability to find more and more planets in the galaxy, then it will become clear that life—and human civilization—is incredibly rare in the galaxy. It's likely that Earth could be the only place where sentient life exists right now in the galaxy, and perhaps even in the universe. Think about that for a moment. In the vast, unimaginable reaches of the universe, this small island home of ours might be the most valuable, unique place. And that would mean that all life on this planet is more rare than anything you can imagine.

We tend to take life for granted. We take life without much thought; we modify living things and beings to our will as a matter of course. We waste and consume without a thought of the astounding uniqueness of every single life form that exists here on Earth.

In the liturgy of Baptism in *The Book of Common Prayer*, we vow to respect the dignity of every human being. Given what we know now about life in the galaxy, this promise takes on a deeper significance and points us toward a different way of living with every living creature that we find in God's earthly creation.

We are created stewards of God's earthly creation. Do we take our job of caring for the rarest thing in the universe seriously?

Do we look after creation as carefully as we do our collections and possessions?

Friday,
Second Week in Lent

The Drake Equation

When the Son of Man comes in his glory,
and all the angels with him,
then he will sit on the throne of his glory.

— Matthew 25:31

When I was teaching astronomy, I always covered the Drake Equation in the last few classes. This equation is a way of estimating the likely number of extraterrestrial civilizations in the universe right now. It won't tell us where they are, or exactly how many there are, but it's an excellent way of thinking about their likelihood. I liked to cover this topic last to keep my students interested in the material and attending the lectures as finals started to draw near.

The equation starts with some broad assumptions about how many galaxies there are, how many stars are in each galaxy, how many stars have planets, how many planets are "earth-like," etc. The numbers in the first couple of variables were pretty well-known. But at the time I was teaching, no one really knew how likely a star was to have planets or how large those possible planets might be. So plugging the numbers into the equation, the answer would vary from saying there was one civilization right now (ours) to saying we lived in a universe teeming with aliens with whom we could talk.

We've gotten a better handle on estimates about the number of stars with planets and how large those might be (more on that tomorrow), but we still don't know the answer to the final parts of the equation: how likely it is that a civilization will arise with whom we could talk right now. That's really the question we're trying to answer. It would be wonderful to know that there had been or would be other life in the universe, but it would be revolutionary to know that we are not alone in the universe and there is someone to talk with.

It strikes me that we sort of know the answer to the final question already. We just haven't been able to prove it. Many people believe in angels. Jesus even implies in Matthew's Gospel that each of us has a guardian angel (Matthew 18:10). The traditional understanding of angels is that they represent another rung on the ladder of creation. They were created by God just as we were. And God's existence itself is another proof for those with faith that we are not alone in the universe.

What does it say about us that there's other life? What does the existence of God and the angels say about our place in the universe, our purpose in creation? Whenever science fiction or theologians speculate on the existence of other life in the universe, they enjoy playing around with the intellectual implications.

How does the existence of God and the angels inform our opinions on the existence of alien life?

What do these answers say about your life?

Saturday, Second Week in Lent

Fermi's Paradox

What is man that you should be mindful of him?
…You have made him but little lower than the angels.

— Psalm 8:5-6

Enrico Fermi, whose name may already be familiar to you as one of the twentieth century's greatest scientists, made an argument that said alien civilizations must be very rare if they even exist at all. His argument, which is deceptively simple, is popularly called Fermi's Paradox.

Essentially Fermi observed that we should expect space-faring aliens to be motivated by the same factors we are: a love of adventure and deep curiosity as well as hope for gain. He believed that if we were able to visit an alien civilization, we would. This is, at its core, an application of the Copernican Principle that we thought about last week. If we are so different from an alien culture that we would explore while they would not, then we must be special in someway, and that would violate the Copernican Principle.

But then Fermi asked, if others would visit us, where are they? That's the big question. Because given that we're a relatively young star, and a relatively young civilization, we can easily imagine that the same natural processes which brought us to this point would have brought other alien civilizations to the same place, and perhaps beyond. So we would expect they'd be looking for someone to talk to, just as we are presently doing. But so far, no one's there.

It's a paradox. They should be there, unless we're very special, but we can't find them. Are they hiding? Why would they do that? Various people have argued they are afraid of us, they are going to attack us, or we are looking in the wrong place. (That last idea doesn't really work; given that we want to be found, we'd expect an alien civilization would want to be found as well.) The other, stronger answer would be to think that it is the nature of intelligent life to destroy itself.

So. What might this paradox say to us about who we are and our place in creation? One of the ways to resolve the paradox that doesn't involve any conspiracy theory or paranoia on our part is to say that we are in fact very rare and very special. That perhaps we are the only civilization in this region of the universe at the moment. And that our future is in danger—particularly if it is indeed the nature of intelligent life to eventually destroy itself.

Jesus prays near the end of his life that we "might all be one" (John 17:21). If we can now realize what Jesus knew already, that we are unique in creation, might we too find a deeper urgency to realize our Savior's dream for us? At the very least, I hope that such a recognition, transcending race and creed, might allow us to transcend what has been used to divide God's children in the past.

How does this simple paradoxical observation change the way we view the world around us?

Does it make us stop to realize how incredibly precious our lives are?

How important is it that we learn to live together?

What steps can we take toward reconciliation?

Third Sunday in Lent

Human Experience and Scale

You will seek the LORD your God,
and you will find him if you search after him
with all your heart and all your soul....
You will return to the LORD your God and heed him.

— Deuteronomy 4:29-30

For the past two weeks, we have been meditating on the structures of the universe that exist on a much larger scale than our typical human experience. We have wondered about the largest structures that can be imagined, and we have contemplated the structures that fill intergalactic and interstellar space. None of these structures are intuitive, or easy to imagine. Most of us, scientists included, imagine them as analogies to what we experience in our everyday human-scaled existence: galaxies as clouds, stars as furnaces, planets as rocks. We don't include the complexities of the electromagnetic fields that fill space. We don't think about the shockwaves pushing glacially through interstellar clouds or the odd behavior of time and space near a black hole or whirling neutron star, because such things are so foreign to our experience that we really can only describe them using the formal language of mathematics.

But this week, I invite you to contemplate the wonder and mystery of creation at our own human scale. I particularly invite you to think about how the air about us has mysterious effects that we can detect but not see—something analogous, according to Jesus, to the way the Holy Spirit behaves. I ask you to try to see everyday things with a fresh perspective, looking for the mystery that each contains, and to find in that mystery an invitation to journey deeper in your pilgrimage to God's fuller presence.

Today, try to look at what has become a common experience in your life and see if you can find something unexpected, something that connects that experience with your own searching for the truth that is God. I believe it is possible to discover a new insight about God by looking at any part of God's created order. Up to this point, I have been inviting you to search in places that are unfamiliar. This week, I invite you to search in the places you know well, but to look particularly at the imprints of God's creative work.

You might not want to limit yourself only to the physical. There is much to be learned by being attentive to your emotional and interior lives too. All of that is part of God's creation as well.

❧

Children have a unique gift to see the world with a freshness we often lose as we age. Can you take an hour today to walk around your neighborhood and see its wonders?

Can you remember the joy you felt when you first encountered a favorite work of art, or music, or literature? What did that moment reveal to you about God's presence in creation?

Monday,
Third Week in Lent

Wind Moves to Fill the Void

The wind blows where it chooses,
and you hear the sound of it,
but you do not know where it comes from
or where it goes.
So it is with everyone who is born of the Spirit.

— John 3:8

The air is constantly moving all about us. We hear it and feel it, but we can't see it. Jesus tells us that the wind is like the Holy Spirit in that we don't know where it has come from or where it is going. But we do know something about what causes the wind.

"Nature abhors a vacuum." That's a short sentence that most of us probably learned as children in science classes. It means that "stuff" wants to move from places where there is more to places where there is less. This is true for water, for gasses, for materials, and even for noncorporeal things like heat. If you have two containers that are somehow connected and allow material a way to move between them, eventually they will both have equal amounts of the material. Anyone who's had a bottle leak into a cooler knows that firsthand.

The wind blows when air moves from a region of high pressure in the atmosphere (often caused by higher temperatures) to a region of low pressure. As the air moves to establish a new equilibrium, the movement of molecules is perceived as the blowing of the wind.

What if Jesus is pointing us to a deep spiritual truth when he connects the Holy Spirit to the experience of the wind? Does the Holy Spirit move from places where there is a great deal of spiritual vitality to places where there is little? Is the Holy Wind of God (in Greek, the word for "spirit" and the word for "wind" are the same) God's way of creating a new beginning for a place that has been dry and desolate?

It has been my experience that prayer changes things. I don't always understand how that happens, but I know prayer makes a difference. And the more people who join in prayer, the bigger the difference. Perhaps we can see the movement of the atmosphere from places of abundance to places that lack as an analogy of what is happening when the Spirit rushes in to make things new. Perhaps it might even be more than just an analogy.

Do you sense the movement of the Holy Spirit in your life right now?

What are you being moved toward, or away from, because of the action of the Spirit?

Are you participating in or resisting that movement?

Tuesday,
Third Week in Lent

The Earth's Tilt, the Sun's Angle

Great are the works of the LORD!
they are studied by all who delight in them.
His work is full of majesty and splendor,
and his righteousness endures forever.
He makes his marvelous works to be remembered.

— Psalm 111:2-4

My bedroom window looks east, across the Narragansett Bay. In the summertime, I wake up with the dawn and watch the sun rise over the horizon, illuminating the bay and the islands. On a warm morning, I'll take my first cup of coffee down to the waterside with me and watch the show from ringside, as it were.

I've watched a number of sunrises over the years, as a camper and hiker, as an astronomer putting the telescopes away after a long night of observing, and now as a person who wakes up far too early in the morning for no good reason. In all of those sunrises, there's something special about the first light of morning. There's a clarity in this light, a purity in the way it illuminates the trees, the leaves, the rocks, even the waves on the water. Artists and photographers know about this special light, and a number of painters have tried various tricks to capture it in oil or watercolor. I've seen a number of astonishingly beautiful attempts, but they all fall short of the experience of the first light of dawn.

Scientifically speaking, this light is unique because the angle the sun makes to the observer is unique. The sun's light travels through more air when the sun is on the horizon than when it shines down from above at noontime. There's a complicated formula for calculating that, but if you remember that the Earth's atmosphere is a thin shell that surrounds the surface of the Earth, you can see why the paths are different at morning, noontime, and evening. The longer pathway through the air has specific effects on the light. It scatters out the blue light (which is why the sky looks rosy at dawn or dusk). It changes the color of the sunlight and changes the way the colors of things in nature appear to our eyes. And when the sun is shining so that things are illuminated from the side, not from above, that seems to highlight textures and shapes differently to our eyes.

The whole effect is due to the Earth rotating on its axis as it revolves around the sun. That rotation and revolution was caused by an unexplained small rotation in the gas cloud that was the nursery for the entire solar system some five billion years ago. Depending upon where you are standing on the surface of the Earth, the result of that rotation and revolution is a yearly cycle of spectacular and breathtaking dawns and dusks. The reason for it is fascinating but not terribly poetic. But describing the result is something that has managed to be just beyond the reach of even the greatest artists and poets.

It strikes me that it can be the other way around when we're talking about God and the things of divinity. The effects of God's creative activity are mostly everyday sorts of things: sunshine, clouds, waves blown by wind on the surface of the waters—all sorts of things that we can explain and that seem very much a part of everyday life. But the first cause, the prime mover of all these, is something that we struggle constantly to imagine, to describe, or to explain. The divine evokes profound responses in each of us, both for good and for ill, and the greatest minds, the most sublime art, and the deepest thinkers have only begun to plumb those experiences.

Or maybe all of it is a part of a whole. The divine is reflected in the majestic rotation of the celestial bodies, in the rosy light of dawn, in the waves and the textures of the bark of the trees. Sometimes it is just a matter of seeing and then looking harder to see more deeply.

Will you pause today to see beyond the first impressions and see the poetry of what is before your eyes?

What do you see?

Wednesday, Third Week in Lent

Oil Refraction Makes Puddle Rainbows

Am I a God nearby, says the LORD, and not a God far off?
...Do I not fill heaven and the earth?

— Jeremiah 23:23-24

Have you ever seen the shimmer of a rainbow on a puddle of water in the street? I don't mean the reflection of a rainbow in the sky, but the much more mundane experience of seeing a puddle of water in the middle of the road and realizing that if you stand in just the right place, you can see a rainbow in the light that is reflected off the surface of the puddle.

You don't normally see the rainbow colors when you look at the surface of a lake or a pond. And you won't typically see them when you look at a puddle in the garden or in the woods. The roadside puddles are really your best bet, because of the oil that collects on the surface of the road dripped by the trucks and autos that stream by every day.

Oil and water don't mix. Motor oil is less dense than water, and will accumulate in a thin film on the surface of the water in the puddle. That thinness gives rise to the rainbow colors.

When light is reflected, the light that bounces off the top of the oil and the light that bounces off the top of the water (below the layer of the oil) travels a slightly different path to our eye. The light that bounces off the water surface goes a little bit further to get to us than the light that bounces off the oil surface. And the angle at which you view the reflection affects the total path difference.

If the path difference is just right, about the same as the wavelength of visible light, the light from the water and the oil surface manages to cancel out all but a single color. As the angle you view changes, the color that is left changes. Hence the rainbow effect.

It's the thinness of the oil film on the puddle that reveals the real colors that make up white light. It strikes me that this is an analogy to the way the "thin" places of the Earth, as the Celtic writers term them, allow us to experience the deeper reality that is all around us. When we are in a place where the separation between the heavenly and earthly realms is narrow or vanishing, we can see the beauty that undergirds our everyday experience. And how poetic in the case of the puddle rainbows, that it is the waste products left behind on the road that makes the place "thin."

Where are the thin places in your life?

What are the places you've been drawing back from because of the waste products you see in that place?

Could it be that you might discover God more completely in that place?

Are you willing to look?

Thursday,
Third Week in Lent

We Are the Pattern

I made the earth, and created humankind upon it;
it was my hands that stretched out the heavens,
and I commanded all their host.

— Isaiah 45:12.

According to medical researchers, the cells in our skeletons live for about seven years and then are replaced. The cells in our skin live about seven weeks. Some cells in our bodies live for years, and some, like red blood cells, live for days. The skeletal cell's lifetime of about seven years, probably the longest lifespan in our body, has given rise to the common idea that we are completely new every seven years or so.

It's clearly more complicated that that; some of our body is new every few days, other parts on the scale of a decade. But the key point is that we are not aware of this constant change. We see the same scars on our skin; we see the same eyes in the mirror; we have a store of memories that goes back to our earliest childhood. The sense of continuity seems to be in direct conflict with the scientific observation of constant biological change.

This particular conundrum highlights an important characteristic of what it means to be human. Our bodies are not permanent, but our patterns are. By patterns, I mean the designs that make our bodies our bodies, determine the shape of our ears, the length of our fingers, the coloring of our eyes. As the natural processes of our body create new cells to take the place of the ones that have died and are being discarded, the information stored in our genes and our DNA instructs them to take the same form, for the most part, as the cells they are replacing.

In other words, you and I are not really bodies that live for seven or eight decades and then wear out and die. We are patterns that are created by the joining of our parents' patterns, given life by the breath we breathe and our other biological processes, and which persist and propagate, in time and space. It's not the body that's at the core of our sense of corporality. It's the pattern.

Thinking of my body as a pattern, as a series of plans, makes it much easier for me to imagine bodily resurrection and life after death. Thinking of the Holy Spirit as the power that gives life to the pattern helps me to understand what the biblical writers are trying to express when they talk about the breath of life. And all of it reminds me that what I perceive as body is much more complicated and profound than what it appears to be.

But it also reminds me that patterns and processes are more than just interesting things with which to divert our minds. They are the core of reality. And God, who according to the Pythagoreans, sang creation into being along with the heavenly choir, is the great patterner of the universe.

⋑

What patterns do you need to be paying more attention to today?

What patterns are causing you to grow toward God?

Which ones are giving you life?

What can you do to focus on those patterns?

Friday,
Third Week in Lent

The Bernoulli Effect Moves a Sailboat

When the Spirit of truth comes,
he will guide you into all the truth.

— John 16:13

I live in Rhode Island on the west side of Narragansett Bay. One of the great things about living on the bay is watching the sailboats move across the waters. Years ago I sailed with friends, and now that I'm living on the water again, I've returned to sailing as a favorite activity.

It's easy to understand how a sailboat moves when the wind is blowing from behind (over the stern). The sails are raised to catch the wind, and the air filling the canvas of the sail pushes the boat forward along with the wind. The more sails that are raised, the faster the boat will go. That's why some boats have more than one mast—it gives them bigger "engines." Moving with the wind behind you is called "running" or "broad reaching"—the words even sound fast.

But there's a bit of controversy about how a sailboat manages to move upwind. It's not possible to sail directly into the wind, but sailing at an angle just off the wind, pointing the bow 30 or 45 degrees off the wind direction, allows the boat to move in a roughly zigzag fashion upwind. Sailing like that is called "tacking" or sailing "close-hauled." Most people say that the boat needs a deep keel (the flat vertical surface of the boat, from bow to stern, that is under the water) to be able to redirect some of the force of the wind on the sail and move the boat. You don't move very fast when you are close-hauled to the wind, but you do move, and if that's the direction you want to go, it's your best option.

The controversy is that there are a number of people who think that close-hauling a boat has less to do with the mechanical work of the keel and more to do with the shape of the cross section of the sail. The cross section of a sail when close-hauled looks very much like the cross section of a bird's wing (or an airplane wing). Because the air moving over the curved portion of the outside of the sail moves more slowly than the air on the inside, there is a higher pressure of air on the inside and a lower pressure of air on the outside— the Bernoulli effect. The higher pressure of air pushes the sail as it tries to move toward the lower pressure.

So, in the case of a sailboat trying to move forward into a strong wind, the only option is to keep the keel beneath the boat, firmly in the water, and let the wind fill the sails.

So too for us in our spiritual lives. When the gales of change are blowing in our lives, we can use a keel to let us steer a course and not just be pushed aside. What might serve as a keel in our lives? If it's analogous to what is present in a boat, it will have to be deep and heavy to keep us on course. Might we imagine that the Holy Scriptures and the traditions of the church could function that way?

~≈~

Where are you finding resistance in your life right now?

How are you trying to move forward in spite of that headwind?

How can scripture and tradition function to counterbalance a lack of equilibrium?

Saturday,
Third Week in Lent

Breathing the Air of Jesus

We, who are many, are one body in Christ,
and individually we are members one of another.

— Romans 12:5

Every breath you take contains something like ten with twenty-three zeros after it molecules of air. That's about a mole of air molecules, if you remember your high school chemistry classes. That's an almost unimaginable number. During a year of our life, we breathe in and out, on average, about ten million times—that's ten with six zeros after it.

Traditionally we believe Jesus lived for thirty-three years during his earthly incarnation, so using the number above, he would have breathed in and out something like 330 million times. Or, assuming he breathed a different set of molecules with each breath (which isn't realistic, but it will work as an approximation), that means that he breathed a total of ten with thirty zeros following molecules of air. That's a very big number, but it only represents about one billionth of the total amount of air on Earth.

But if you work out all the math, it turns out that each breath we take contains many of the same air molecules that Jesus breathed during his lifetime. You and I are literally, with each breath, breathing the same air as Our Lord. And, by extension, the same air that was breathed by every saint, known and unknown, who ever lived—and every sinner as well. You are breathing the air of Jesus mixed with the air that Judas Iscariot breathed. Every time you inhale.

You can even work out how many of the molecules in one of your breaths was a part of Jesus' last breath on the cross. It's not many, maybe one or two out of the many, many molecules you breathe, but there are a few. And there are a few of the last breaths of Caesar Augustus, of Leonardo da Vinci, of Queen Elizabeth, of everyone who has ever lived. With each breath you take, you are physically connected to everyone who has ever lived on the planet.

One of the simplest forms of physical prayer is to quiet yourself, try to empty your mind, and focus on each breath you take. If you can carve out a few minutes today, try to pray this way, to be aware, be conscious of the deep connectedness of all human life throughout all of our history. The air of laughter, of tears, of heroes, and of scoundrels surrounds us at every moment of our lives, filling our lungs and giving us life.

❧

Have you ever imagined that you were praying when you were just sitting still and breathing? If not, could you try to pray that way today?

You are not just connected to the great heroes of history when you breathe—you are connected to the scoundrels and the traitors as well. Take some time to reflect on how the act that gives us life brings us into intimate relationship with all manner and conditions of humanity.

Fourth Sunday in Lent

Learning to See

Do you have eyes, and fail to see?

— Mark 8:18

When I was a child and active in Cub Scouts, my parents bought me a subscription to *Boy's Life,* a magazine connected with the scouting movement in the United States. It was full of all sorts of interesting articles, had a few cartoon strips in the back, and talked a great deal about what the character of a Boy Scout was supposed to be.

One of the articles that I still remember was a short story about a young surfer who had befriended a Buddhist monk. The surfer was asked by his friend if he would mind if the friend came along with him to the beach every morning during the summer school vacation. The monk intended to sit on the cliffs overlooking the beach and meditate on the meaning of surfing while watching the surfers.

The young man in the story was happy for the company, but he tried to get the monk to not keep his distance from the surfers. He wanted him to get on the board with him and experience the act of surfing. It was only in the experience, the surfer argued, that the monk would be able to understand. But the monk was insistent about his desire to understand the act of surfing by meditating rather than doing. He tried to explain to the young man that such meditation would allow him to learn how to surf as well.

This was a wonder to the young man. The monk insisted that if he were allowed to meditate for the entire summer about the young man's surfing, by the end of the summer he would be as good a surfer as the young man. And in the story, that's exactly how it played out. There was a moment of climactic wonder when, on a cool, late August morning, the monk finally came down the steps to the water's edge, took the board out to the breakers, and stood up without hesitation, riding a beautiful wave all the way into the beach.

There were, I'm sure, many levels of meaning in that story. But the idea that impressed me then, and impresses me still, was the author's point that there is little or nothing we cannot achieve if we will learn to truly see what is happening before us.

Forty Days of Lent

During this fourth week of Lent, I invite you to meditate with me on what it means to see, to change our perspective and expand our understanding of our experience of creation. If you can, today in particular, pay close attention to one thing, one small thing in your daily routine, for a while. Look closely to see it with a new set of eyes; look for the wonder in the actions.

Our church liturgy is an excellent place to start. Perhaps today you might pay attention to the flickering of the candle on the altar, or the movement of the priest's hands during the celebration of the Eucharist. Or perhaps you might look to see the deeper significance of the relationships we have with one another in the moment that the congregation stops to share the peace with one another.

Take a few moments today to look for God's hand in a natural object today—a rock or a plant or something you notice that interests you. What can you recognize about God as you do this?

Monday,
Fourth Week in Lent

Learning to Be Aware

Be still, then, and know that I am God.

— Psalm 46:11

I remember hearing the former Archbishop of Canterbury Rowan Williams being asked about the meaning and practice of prayer. In his response, he said—as he has said in other places—that one of the ways to pray is to simply sit still, knowing that you are in the presence of God, and to listen with your whole body to hear what God might be saying. The Archbishop even described the sensation that occurs when one is engaged in that sort of prayer as the experience of your ears, your hearing, growing beyond the limits of your body.

The practice of prayer as a form of attentiveness isn't unique to Christianity. You can find other faiths, philosophers, and spiritual guides suggesting that we need to meditate, to pray by being conscious, by being aware. But the fact that intentional awareness to God's creation and creative activity isn't unique to our faith doesn't mean we ought to neglect it. Rather, it seems to me that its universality is a sign we ought to be taking the activity very seriously.

So today, try to take a few moments to still yourself and to listen. Perhaps you'll want to give the busy, active part of your brain something to do so that it doesn't keep trying to derail your intention to be attentive. Some people use the rosary as a way of keeping their attention focused. Others might pray the "Jesus Prayer" (*Lord Jesus Christ, Son of God, have mercy on me, a sinner.*). Some people repeat the Lord's Prayer again and again as they breathe. Or maybe you find that just being still is what you need.

However you still yourself, be aware of the mystery of your body. Listen. Feel the breaths that give you life entering and leaving your body. Feel the beats of your heart that circulate the small living creatures that feed and maintain the colonies of life in your body that make you who you are. Listen to the ringing in your ears that is caused by the tiny waving of the hairs in your inner ear. If your stomach rumbles, think on the colonies of bacteria in your gut that influence our lives and our moods in ways that we're just coming to understand.

You, and all of the life structures that work cooperatively to make your body your own self, are marvelously made. And in our daily life we can easily become too busy to hear, to feel, to pray upon the wonder of our existence. For a few moments today, be aware of your body and give thanks and praise in your prayer.

Have you ever tried to pray by moving your body?

What can you hear of God in the small rhythms of your breath?

Forty Days of Lent

Tuesday, Fourth Week in Lent

Optical Afterimages

I lift up my eyes...

— Psalm 121:1

I had a few moments this morning for quiet prayer in the nave of a church. It's a particularly lovely building with justly famous stained glass windows. As I was settling and quieting myself before beginning my prayers, I spent a few minutes gazing at the windows, letting the colors, the shapes, and the stories wash over me. The church is oriented toward the east, so the altar window was filled with morning light. As the sun moved slowly across the sky, its light would catch the bevels and joints in the stained glass, creating a shower of sparkles and flashes. It was a beautiful, slow journey across the window.

I knelt down in the pew, and as I closed my eyes to begin my prayers, I could "see" the image of the altar window. I could see how the structural parts of the window created a cross and how the shape of the window naturally drew my attention to the altar. And I noticed that, to my surprise, the colors were even more vivid.

What filled my vision that morning was an afterimage. This effect was caused by the parts of my eye that are used to see color becoming over-whelmed by the intense light of the sun shining through the stained glass. The cells in the retina were still sending a signal to my brain that I was continuing to see, even with closed eyes—not with great detail, but with blocks of colors that high-lighted the shape and structure I had missed seeing because of the intensity of the light.

It struck me that my experience of seeing the afterimage—seeing something that was obscured from my regular sight—is a parable on the act of prayer. There are moments in prayer when God's presence is so intense and real that it can overwhelm all of our senses. Those moments are rare, at least for me, but when they happen, I want to be as still as possible because I want to remain in that "place," in the presence of God. And when the moment has passed, and I open my eyes and reengage with creation, I do so with a sort of an afterimage filling my heart. I still "see" the presence of God, but in a different way, and in a way that helps me to see the world around me differently. I can see how God's actions create structures and forms in creation and in our relationships. I can see the colors of God's love in a way that I missed when I was dazzled by the fleeting sense of God's nearness.

Usually when I finish my prayers, I'm reluctant to reengage the world around me. But this morning, as I meditated on the effects of the afterimage, I realized that I shouldn't be reluctant. I ought to be eager, particularly so if the moments of prayer are profound and I am deeply aware of God's presence. Because it's those prayers that leave the afterimage on my heart that will allow me to see the world with new eyes and to be able to recognize things I hadn't noticed before.

What afterimage do you see in your prayer today?

How long did it last?

What is God trying to tell you in it?

Wednesday,
Fourth Week in Lent

Violin Cathedral

May the God of hope fill you with all joy and peace.

— Romans 15:13

A series of pictures I came across recently show images taken inside musical instruments. There are pictures taken inside organ pipes, piano cabinets, clarinets, and others. The most arresting image to me was taken inside of an old violin that had been crafted by a famous master violin maker.

The way the image is lit, you can see the light pouring through the scrollwork holes on the front of the violin. The light makes it possible to see the grain of the wood, the shadows, the joinery, and even the label inside the instrument. There's a modern minimalist beauty to the image. It's very architectural in appearance. If you didn't know what you were seeing, you might imagine you were looking at an empty concert or lecture hall. I thought that when I first saw the picture.

But as I looked at it and meditated on the beauty, I was struck by the emptiness of the space. There is a void at the heart of every great string instrument— a beautiful, finely crafted hole that is the key to the music that the instrument was created to make. It's the empty space with its unique shape and material construction that gives voice to the music an artist creates using the instrument. The void, the lack, the empty space at the core is, in some ways, the reason the instrument works. Without that shape, the small, quiet sounds made by drawing horsehair across gut strings wouldn't be amplified, shaped, and colored into a melody that fills the room and our hearts.

The empty place is the essence of the instrument.

⚬

What empty places do you have within you?

Could it be that God is using those voids in your inner life—the negative spaces of your prayer life—to make music you only barely perceive but that makes the hearts of other people sing?

Thursday,
Fourth Week in Lent

Butterflies and the Missing Mountain

Do not be conformed to this world,
but be transformed by the renewing of your minds,
so that you may discern what is the will of God—
what is good and acceptable and perfect.

— Romans 12:2

Monarch butterflies are known for their annual migration across the continent of North America. In October, they move southward from Canada to central Mexico to survive the cold of winter, and then in the spring begin the return northward to spend the summer in the Canadian climate. One of the marvels of this migration is that the lifespan of the butterfly is so short that a single individual cannot complete the whole journey. There will be four successive generations of butterflies between the leaving and the returning, year in and year out.

But even more marvelous to me is that as the butterflies travel southward they fly over Lake

Superior before entering the United States. For no apparent reason, they cross the lake in one non-stop flight, heading not north to south but south to east to south again. It's an extraordinarily odd path to choose, given their size and the ardors of the journey. They really don't have to cross the lake at all, and they certainly don't need to take that eastward jog over the open water.

The best explanation for their behavior is that the same mechanism that imprinted the yearly journey's path in the instinctive behavior of generations of monarch butterflies has also imprinted the memory that, long before the last ice age, there was an enormous mountain looming where Lake Superior is now. The butterflies are wheeling around the base of the mountain that no longer exists.

The butterflies are still avoiding a long-gone obstacle because even though they can see it is no longer there, they cannot change their instinctive behavior. The mountain has been gone for a very long time, yet the behavior and migratory path have not yet changed. Perhaps the mechanism that imprinted the instinctive path is no longer functional, having served its evolutionary purpose.

Perhaps there's some key environmental condition missing that keeps the journey from being reset.

No matter the reason, two things are evoked in me as I contemplate this behavior. The first is that we can see, or at least be aware of, the mountain's former existence, not by looking at the geological record but by watching how life today behaves. There is an imprint of that mountain in a place we'd least expect it to be found. It is only by careful observation and questioning that we can make sense of this otherwise senseless, profligate behavior by the butterflies.

The second is that the butterflies are trapped in a behavior that does them no good because they have no way to communicate to successive generations that their "map" is no longer useful. They learn that what was there is there no longer, but have not found the way to share that information.

❧

How many times do we learn something new about what it is to be human in our moment of history and either do not think to or cannot find a way to share this insight?

What can you do to change this behavior in yourself?

Friday,
Fourth Week in Lent

Light Pressure Spins a Wheel

Send out your light and your truth, that they may lead me.

—— Psalm 43:3

When I was a boy, one of my friends had a glass bulb on his windowsill that had a small paddle wheel in the middle of it. The paddle wheel was mounted on a pin. There were four blades on the paddle, with one side of each blade painted black and the other side painted white. The wheel was constantly spinning. Perhaps you've seen one of these?

I noticed that the wheel would spin the fastest when the sunlight was the strongest. Noontime was quite the show. And as darkness fell, the wheel would slow down, barely turning at all. My friend told me that the light shining on the blades was making the wheel turn. It certainly seemed to be what was happening. But even then, I knew enough about light to wonder how something that had no mass was able to hit something and make it move.

The proper name of the device on my friend's window shelf is a Crookes' Radiometer. It was invented by chemist Sir William Crookes in the latter part of the nineteenth century as an offshoot of some work he was doing in carefully weighing research samples. Most of the radiometers sold in gift shops have a very weak vacuum within the bulb. But a properly made one, with a hard vacuum, can put on quite a show when it is exposed to even a little bit of light.

Some people have argued that the blades move because of light pressure—a real effect that is caused when the massless photons strike a surface, giving up their energy in a form of momentum transfer. But this effect, while present, is too small to cause what is observed. And, it was discovered, the blades will turn the other direction if you take the bulb out of the hot sun and place it in a refrigerator, cooling the entire assembly.

It turns out that the spinning is primarily caused by the heating and cooling of the surface of the blades. As they are heated, the blades force the particles that are near them to move away. By Newton's third law, the reaction force causes the blade to move in the other direction. The explanation (and there's more to it than that, of course) was something that Einstein first proposed. A second effect, called thermal transpiration, also contributes to the motion.

What's inspiring to me is that the radiometer moves simply by being placed into the bright light. And the motion is more pronounced the stronger the void is around the wheel. It makes me think of our own prayer lives. Sometimes, when we are motionless or adrift, what we really need to do is find a place filled with light. Just being placed in the bright light is often enough to get us to move forward. And I'm rather taken that the deeper the sense of something lacking, the stronger the effect becomes when the object is placed in the light. Perhaps that's true too for us. The more we feel the lack of God's presence in our lives, the more the light of God's presence can move us when we come into its presence.

Where is the place of God's light in your life right now?

What needs to change so that you can be more fully illuminated?

Saturday,
Fourth Week in Lent

Molecules Look Like We Thought

Two are better than one,
because they have a good reward for their toil.

— Ecclesiastes 4:9

Recently there was a technical breakthrough that, for the first time, allows us to take "pictures" of molecules. Prior to this, because of the small size of atoms and the relatively larger size of visible light, we used electrons or other short wavelength particles to bombard and then reconstruct what we were observing. The problem was that, even using tools like this, we still couldn't see the molecule in any detail—we could make out only the size of the molecules and how they were arranged with each other.

But this new technique, called an atomic force microscope, allows scientists to see a single molecule with a resolution of a nanometer (one billionth of a meter). The technique also allows us to distinguish between single, double, and triple bonds between atoms in a molecule. (A bond is created by two atoms sharing an electron. A single bond is one shared electron, a double is two shared electrons, etc.) For the first time, we're able to see the actual structures and mechanisms that molecules use to maintain their integrity.

The really startling find in all of this is that the molecules look just like the simple schematics we learned to draw in junior high chemistry class. Do you remember making molecular models using styrofoam balls and pipe cleaners? Or maybe your school lab had one of the fancy sets with wooden atoms whose predrilled holes forced you to make bonds at specific angles between the atoms? They were used to show the structure of a water molecule or simple gasses like carbon dioxide and ozone. These were intended to be only schematic representations, but according to the new observations, molecules really look just like this. To me the most impressive new image I saw was the picture of an actual benzene ring—which looked just like we imagined, with alternating single and double bonds and all.

I find myself reflecting on the power of our imagination in all of this. Together, we imagined a way to describe the structure of a part of nature we could not see, either directly or indirectly. We tried to guess, based on secondary evidence, how things might go together. And it turns out that by using our imagination, we were able to correctly understand the basis of chemical bonding. I'm also struck that this work of imagination was a community effort. Ideas were shared, critiqued, and refined. It wasn't the work of a single individual; it was the collective imagination of the community of scientists who were able to correctly describe the molecular realm.

What does it mean to think and wonder about God in the context of community?

Could our wondering and imagining about God and the activity of God in creation be uncovering truth in the same way as it has in chemistry?

Fifth Sunday in Lent

The Quantum Realm

For we know only in part, and we prophesy only in part.

— 1 Corinthians 13:9

In this last week of Lent, we turn our attention to the strange, totally counterintuitive realm of creation that is governed by quantum physics. For the past few weeks we have been meditating on effects and phenomena that are, for the most part, things we have all experienced. But as we shrink the scale down to the lengths even smaller than the radius of an atom, we find that it is almost impossible to imagine what we find to be true.

A basic question has occupied natural philosophy almost from the beginning. Is there a thing that is too small to be divided? Democritus, an ancient Greek philosopher, thought that there had to be. He called the imagined indivisible things "atoms," from the Greek word that means literally "uncuttable." He imagined that such things must be eternal, since, by their very indivisible nature, they must be indestructible. Initially he and his students thought that atoms gave the things we see and touch their nature. Sharp things contained sharp atoms; sweet things contained many sweet atoms. But it turns out that his ideas were just a little off.

When scientists first recognized the existence of atoms, they thought they had discovered the entities that Democritus imagined. But atoms can be divided. It's the things that make up atoms that turn out to be "atomic" in the way that the early philosophers imagined. The electrons, the quarks, and other fundamental elementary particles were created in the fires of the Big Bang explosion that began the universe and exist, each one unchanged, still today. Everything you are made of is a product of the first moments of the explosive expansion of the universe. The electrons and quarks may have lived in the core of some ancestral star until they were knit together in their present arrangements that, for example, we call a carbon or iron atom, which were then knit again in recent earthly experience into a sugar molecule or a knife blade.

And for reasons no one understands, all of those fundamental particles are exactly the same. Each up or down quark has exactly the same mass and charge. Each electron is exactly like any other electron. There is no variation, no fuzziness. They are all identical quanta.

And to make matters more complicated, they have an inherent duality that stretches our ability to comprehend past its limit. Each particle is also a wave. Each wave is also a particle. And there are experiments that can only be explained by imagining the electron is a particle colliding with another, and there are experiments that can only be explained by imagining that each electron is a wave interfering with another. It's all very strange.

God is something like all of this. There are moments when we experience God and we think we can understand. It would seem that God is like us, just larger and more powerful. But then something happens—a miracle, or a disaster, or a prophecy that suddenly turns our understanding of God upside down and makes us realize that everything that has gone before in our experience of the divine is incomplete and, in some fundamental ways, misleading.

In this coming week, as we meditate on the odd, counterintuitive qualities of the quantum realm, see if you can also be aware of experiences of the divine that simply won't fit into any of your categories of what God is supposed to be like. That mismatch doesn't mean there isn't a God, any more than the odd behavior of the fundamental particles doesn't mean they can't exist. It means that what we think we know, we know only in part.

~~~~~~

What is fundamental about God for you?

What are the very simplest things you can say about God?

Monday,
Fifth Week in Lent

Uncertainty

For now we see in a mirror, dimly,
but then we will see face to face.
Now I know only in part;
then I will know fully,
even as I have been fully known.

— 1 Corinthians 13:12

It's funny how we as a society have come to believe science can answer any question in a definitive way. It doesn't matter what someone might claim. What matters, at least in popular culture, is what "scientists now say." The idea that there is one correct answer and that science alone has the ability to determine what that answer is comes, I think, from the way most of us are exposed to the scientific method as students. Generally we are shown how to solve problems using specific tools and are expected to be as accurate as possible. When I was teaching physics, it wasn't uncommon for a student to think that if an answer to three decimal places was good, then an answer to ten (the limit of the calculator used) was better.

But the truth is that every answer in scientific research has an associated uncertainty. Every numeric measurement has an associated error. A good experiment is designed to minimize those errors as much as possible, but there's a limit to what can be done. At best we are limited by the precision and accuracy of the instruments we are using to make a measurement. Because of that, there are a number of formal techniques to account for the various errors in a measurement, ways to accumulate them and then graphically show them when data is presented. In some fields the "error bars," as they're called, are small. In some fields, like astronomy, the errors can be 200 or 300 percent of the measured quantity.

Even if we could somehow magically minimize those sorts of extreme errors, there is, inherent in reality itself, a fundamental uncertainty at all levels. You may have heard of the Heisenberg Uncertainty principle. That principle is a consequence of the experimental observation that all particles have an associated wavelength and wave behavior. It means that it is impossible to ever know everything about even the simplest part of the universe. An electron is a very small, unusually simple, mostly well-understood part of the universe, and yet, if you try to tell me exactly where it is, you forfeit the ability to tell me anything about its motion. The situation is worse for even slightly more complicated systems, and in terms of absolute knowledge, it's unimaginably difficult for something massive.

Truth, scientifically speaking, just isn't the absolute we want it to be. The best any of us can do is an approximation, a best estimate, of the answer to a simple question. Keeping that in mind causes me to hold my truths lightly, as former Presiding Bishop Frank Griswold used to say. What I think I know, I can only ever know in part. I can only see through a mirror, dimly.

But I do have reason to hope that eventually, in another moment, I shall be able to see the whole of the truth.

≈

What truth might you need to hold more lightly so that you can love your neighbor more fully?

Tuesday,
Fifth Week in Lent

A Ladder to God

All things came into being through him,
and without him not one thing came into being.

— John 1:3

Years ago, physicists started trying to organize all the many varieties of subatomic particles in ways that they hoped would let them discern a pattern. They wanted to see if this organization would make it clear where they ought to look to find new particles or to identify which particles were the most fundamental ones found in nature.

If you group the electron and the quarks that make up the neutron and proton (the up quark and the down quark) and the neutrino (a small neutral particle that is important in radioactive decay, among other things), you can see a sort of family of subatomic particles that are responsible for the vast majority of ordinary matter. You can then group three more particles—the muon, the charm quark, and the strange quark—with a neutrino flavor that seems to be associated with the muon, and you get a parallel family of particles that make up a big chunk of the more exotic matter we see in high energy physics. And if you take this all one step further, grouping the tauon and the top quark and the bottom quark with the tau neutrino, you get a family that seems to constitute the most difficult to find or observe particles—particles that exist only in very, very extreme circumstances.

When you look at the three families of particles, and arrange them in terms of mass energy from lightest (the electron family) to the heaviest (the tauon family), you get a sort of ladder. And there's no reason to think that the ladder doesn't have heavier rungs above the tauon family. It would seem likely, in fact, that if we had the ability to create even more extreme high temperature and pressure conditions in Earth-bound laboratories, we'd find more families above these. Perhaps countless numbers of families…

It's all very reminiscent of the dream Jacob had the night he slept on the ground in the place he named Bethel (described in Genesis 28:10-22). Jacob saw a ladder extending all the way up into heaven with angels ascending and descending upon it. Rank upon rank of angels up to God, and rank upon rank of angels from God to humankind.

I wonder if we might look at the created order all around us today and see in it the very first rung or rungs of the ladder that leads us up to God. Everything we see in our everyday life has a rung of things above it, and there's at least one more rung above that. God, who is light and energy, fills all levels of the creation, and even beyond that. The things of our existence can be stepping stones on our journey to God's fuller presence.

Anyone who has been inspired by the physical fabric of a beautiful worship space or awed by an expansive vista knows exactly how this happens.

～

What are you seeking to simplify in your life?

Is there something in your life that might be more complex than you want it to be?

Can you accept that?

Wednesday,
Fifth Week in Lent

Entanglement

*We know that all things work together for good
for those who love God.*

— Romans 8:28

Years ago I decided to name my blog "Entangled
States." It has turned out to be a perfect choice
for a number of reasons, most of which I hadn't
anticipated. I chose the name to make a point
to people who were making assertions about
theology and using nature to support them. I'm
totally supportive of using our observations of the
mechanisms which undergird God's creation to
reason our way to deeper understandings of God's
purposes, but I wanted to caution people that doing
so could be a double-edged sword.

The phenomenon of quantum entanglement
is very hard for us to imagine. It's relatively easy
to describe mathematically, but because it occurs
at the very smallest scales of existence, it's not

something we experience. Entanglement happens when the wave natures of two particles begin to influence each other as a result of the particles' shared history—something like a collision usually. Once the particles are entangled, changes to one particle cause a change to the other.

That's not terribly surprising, of course. We're all familiar with that happening. Think of a long line of dominoes set close to each other. Knock one domino down, and they will all eventually fall. But they fall because they come into contact with each other. In the quantum phenomenon, the two particles were once in "contact" with each other, but even after they are separated, if one "falls down" the other one will too. Einstein called this sort of thing "spooky action at a distance." He spent a great deal of time trying to prove that it wasn't so, because if it is, some of the fundamental underpinnings of classical physics (upon which both Newton and Einstein built) are incorrect.

In the latter part of the twentieth century, a long series of different experiments showed that Einstein was wrong in this instance. The spooky-action-at-a-distance behavior between entangled systems is a fundamental phenomenon of physics.

It's been observed at length scales that are nearly comprehensible to humans, and it appears to be critically important in photosynthesis (the mechanism that plants use to covert sunlight into food). But there's no way to explain it using classical enlightenment-based thinking. Understanding entanglement requires us to create new categories of thought and give up some of the basic assumptions that we've been using for many centuries.

Theology and physics are both parts of philosophy, and if one system changes the way it works, there are ramifications for the other. If we somehow managed to physically prove the existence of the divine, we'd have to rework large sections of physics (and do some patching up of theology too). I believe the relationship works the other way as well. If we discover something fundamental about the way the universe is connected, then we have to rework some of our understandings of theology. That work is just getting started, by the way.

But even while that work progresses, we can meditate on the concept of entanglement. A change to one part of the system changes the rest of the system, even when we can't understand how or by what mechanism. A change to a community affects all of its members. A change to our understanding of God changes the way we see our place in creation. A change to our understanding of what is required to do justice changes the ways we live together within the church.

How has your understanding of things, of events, of concepts in your life, changed the way you live and the things you do?

Thursday,
Fifth Week in Lent

Bell's Theorem

Trust in the LORD with all your heart,
and do not rely on your own insight.

— Proverbs 3:5

Yesterday I mentioned that Albert Einstein was very uncomfortable with the way quantum physics allowed for two particles to communicate at a distance from each other through no obvious means. He termed the phrase "spooky-action-at-a-distance" to poke fun at the idea. It was an important issue for Einstein, because one of the great successes of his theory of general relativity was to explain away the apparent action-at-a-distance issues that were contained in Newton's gravitational laws. For example, we know that the Earth is aware of the gravity of the sun, but we don't know how. Unlike a cork floating in a river, moving with the current because the water molecules push it along, there's no matter contact in gravitation. It was Einstein's great insight that we could explain how the Earth "sensed" the sun's gravity by thinking about gravity as curving the space and time that the Earth was moving in. The Earth doesn't know the sun is acting at a great distance from it, but it senses the curvature of space and time around it and moves along that curved pathway.

When Einstein thought about the behavior of entangled particles, he became convinced that the action-at-a-distance theory was incomplete. There must be something more basic happening, just as he had found in the situation with gravity. And so he, and many others, worked to uncover that more fundamental understanding and to explain the "scandal" that quantum physics was causing.

But in the late 1960s, a scientist/mathematician named John Bell found a way to test whether a theory was missing some deeper insights. Bell argued that if his test could be carried out on a quantum system, it would indicate that Einstein was right, that there was more to the situation, and that the quantum claims represented an incomplete understanding. People worked for years to create an experiment that would test Bell's Theorem. And when it was tested, the results indicated that Einstein and his collaborators were wrong. There was nothing incomplete about quantum mechanics. It was the classical understanding of causation that was mistaken.

No one particularly liked the result, because it called into question some of our most basic assumptions about how the universe works. But it's been verified again and again, and Bell's thinking has been repeatedly analyzed and so far has withstood all challenges. What this means to us is that the way in which we "know" the world works isn't actually correct. There are strange, counterintuitive physical laws that are the real rules. Because of our size and timescale, we tend to miss all of that.

And this means that absolutes—yes and no answers, even a desire for certainty about the most basic questions—do not exist. In terms of the created order, the only absolute that exists is that there are no other absolutes.

In Anglican moral theology, there is a famous dictum that "circumstances alter cases." Moral judgments are very rarely ever absolute because of this. We can struggle to find the best answer to a question, but never "the" answer.

As you continue your faith journey through Lent, think about this concept in terms of your life and actions, and reflect on the choices you make knowing that there are no absolutes.

How much of your desire to judge yourself and others comes from a desire to do the right thing?

What if it was impossible to ever absolutely know the right thing to do?

How would that change your thinking about yourself or of your sinfulness?

And just as importantly, how would it change your thinking about your neighbor, or your enemy?

Friday,
Fifth Week in Lent

The Emptiness at the Heart

O Lord, how manifold are your works!
In wisdom you have made them all;
the earth is full of your creatures.
Yonder is the great and wide sea
with its living things too many to number,
creatures both small and great.

— Psalm 104:25-26

As you look more carefully at things, you will see more and more details emerge. Perhaps you have spent time peering through a microscope and been amazed at what wonders begin to appear as you increase the magnification. As a child, I was always astonished by what I could discover living in a single drop of water from a puddle.

But something unexpected happens as you look at smaller and smaller scales. Unexpected features give way to cellular life, cells give way to gigantic biological molecules, then smaller ones, then atoms, and then, well, nothing. Once we get to the atomic level, and start to look at what exists inside the electron cloud of an atom, we discover that the inside of an atom is pretty much completely without structure. I don't mean that there isn't a core, a nucleus, but that the nucleus of an atom is so small, something like 100,000 times smaller than the electron cloud, that essentially—and unexpectedly—atoms are empty space.

It's that emptiness, that void within all atomic matter, that makes me stop and take notice. If we lived somehow at such a length scale, our experience of reality would be profoundly different. If we did, the next nearest person to us would be as far away as the moon is from the center of the Earth. Between the two people would be, well, nothing. And the next thing beyond that person would be another moon away.

In such an environment, there would be no detail, no wild kaleidoscope of creation, no puzzles, no complication. Just silent emptiness. There would be nothing for us to try to understand, nothing for us to see as an analogy of something else. There would be little or nothing that would make us wonder why. It would be only the nothingness that would point us toward God. And I don't know if that would be enough.

When I imagine living in such a sterile vacuum of existence, I find myself grateful for the crowded, noisy world that is my everyday experience. It causes me to wonder, to strive, to look for connections. The confusion of the world leads me to wonder about the author of the confusion. And that leads me to wonder about God.

Could you try to see the hectic confusion you encounter today, not as a distraction from God, but as rungs on a ladder that lead you to God?

What are you grateful for in the crowded, noisy world of your everyday experience?

Saturday,
Fifth Week in Lent

Observation Changes the System

Do not worry about anything, but in everything
by prayer and supplication with thanksgiving
let your requests be made known to God.
And the peace of God,
which surpasses all understanding,
will guard your hearts and your minds in Christ Jesus.

— Philippians 4:6-7

One of the surprising tenets of quantum physics is the idea that when we observe something, we change it. The idea itself is not terribly surprising. Anyone who has put a cold cooking spoon into a pot of boiling water knows that the moment you put the spoon into the water, the character of the rolling boil is interrupted, both by the cold temperature of the spoon and the way the surface of the spoon changes the movement of the convection in the water. If you were to put a big thermometer into the water to try to measure its temperature, you could see how that would have the same effect on the system. The thermometer is going to be at a different temperature from the water, and it's going to take a little bit of time for the thermometer and the water in the pot to meet in the thermal middle. And the introduction of a rigid object into the currents of the boiling water will affect the way the water is moving—probably reducing the energy of the boiling.

The surprising thing would be to use a medical thermometer, the kind you stick in your ear to measure your temperature when you're sick. If you were to point such a gadget (after modifying it, of course) at a pot of boiling water, you'd be able to measure the temperature of the water by measuring the sort of light emitted by the thermal energy of the water. It's hard to see how that measurement would change the way the water was boiling. But if you play with the idea for a bit, you can begin to recognize that some of the thermal energy that is measured will also be reflected back to the water, thus raising its temperature ever so slightly.

On a large (macroscopic) scale, we generally ignore such a small change. But if we're working with a much smaller system, something on the quantum scale, then reflecting back one or two of the photons carrying away the energy of a much simpler, smaller system would obviously have a much larger effect. It would be a change we wouldn't be able to ignore.

This isn't actually what we mean when we talk about the "observer effect" in quantum physics, which has to do with the way that a probability wave (something that describes how a system is evolving in time) "collapses" as soon as the system is "measured." Prior to the measurement, we can only speak about the probabilities that the system is doing one thing or another. As soon as we measure the system, we pin it into an observed state. It's an odd, counterintuitive, not understood phenomenon.

I've always found a parallel here with the way I imagine prayer works: when we pray, we imagine something is happening because we are praying. There are times in my prayer when I know that my prayer is changing me more than my prayer is changing the situation I am raising up to God. There are times in my prayers when I am made more aware that God is present in the situation because I am praying. But there are times when

I wonder if my very act of prayer might have an effect on a system in the same way that observing a system has an effect. I don't understand it, I can't explain it, but it does give me something to wonder about.

Physicists will admit, if you ask them, that no one really knows what it physically means to make an observation on a small system. We can talk about the mathematics, but we can't connect the mathematics and what physically happens. That seems parallel to what happens with theologians when they talk about prayer. We know that Jesus tells us to pray. We know that prayer changes things. But we don't always understand how.

Maybe, if you're worrying about what happens when you pray, you might remember that even though we don't understand how something works, it still works.

Have you ever felt the prayers of others in your life?

What was that like?

What changed as a result?

Sunday of the Passion: Palm Sunday

Mysteries

His disciples did not understand these things at first.

— John 12:16

The liturgy of many congregations on Palm Sunday begins with the reenactment of Jesus' triumphal entry into Jerusalem—with the distribution and blessings of palms and often a physical procession through the parish neighborhood that ends with people entering the church singing some of their favorite hymns. But just as soon as we settle ourselves in the pews, we begin to read lessons that direct us toward the shocking, heartrending events of Holy Week: stories of betrayal, abandonment, rejection, torture, and death. What began with joy and excitement quickly turns to pathos and horror as we read the story of the Passion narrative.

How such a shift could happen so quickly has always seemed to me one of the hardest parts of Holy Week to understand. It is too much for some scholars, who argue that the crowds could not have changed from adulation to condemnation so quickly, so therefore the traditional narrative must be collapsing a larger span of time into a shorter one for dramatic effect. But it is really only a week. And crowds are notorious for turning on people. Perhaps it is not so hard to imagine.

But still, that God allowed this to happen seems to me a great mystery. And that word, mystery, runs throughout all the events of Holy Week. So this week I ask you to contemplate the great mysteries, not only of the Passion narrative, but also of the natural sciences and even theology. There is much we can say with confidence about the world that God has created. But there is much more that we know little about or have even seen hinted at. Perhaps by remembering how surrounded we are by mystery, even in the most successful human intellectual endeavors, we will be less scandalized by the mysteries at the heart of Jesus' death and resurrection.

Meditate on the mysteries in the Passion narrative and in the natural world. What is the meaning of mystery?

Why is it that mystery so often makes us uncomfortable?

Monday in Holy Week

How Can Matter Exist?

*...so that they may have all the riches of assured
understanding and have the knowledge of God's mystery,
that is, Christ himself, in whom are hidden
all the treasures of wisdom and knowledge.*

— Colossians 2:1-3

When I taught physics, the final series of my lectures
focused on the great failures of modern physics. I
didn't want my students to imagine that the work
was done or science was successful in everything
it did. In this I was inspired by my advisor for my
Master's degree in general relativity theory, who
constantly reminded us that the equations we
were studying, as beautiful as they were, were
still riddled with flaws. He did this to inspire us
to be continually searching for new avenues into
a deeper understanding of problems that many
people imagined were solved and completed.

Scientists know that trying to describe the
actual detailed mechanisms at work in creation is
much too complicated in most cases. We have had

the most success where we have been able to simplify the situation to make it physically unrealistic but mathematically solvable. Quantum mechanics is an excellent example: Most of the work done in describing the behavior of particles moving in a semiconductor structure (like the transistor at the heart of any microprocessor) is based on the most simplistic ideas you can imagine. That makes the math easy enough that we can solve the equation.

But we can lose sight of the structures we build upon, at least until we are forced to recognize that our simplistic models require us to imagine impossible things. Take the electron, one of the simplest particles known. Every electron is exactly like every other electron—all carry the same electrical charge, all have the same mass, all have the same "spin." The simplest model that we have to describe them is of a small ball with charge distributed across its surface. The balls whiz around in space-time, bouncing off one another and other particles, like little balls rolling around on a table.

But this creates a problem when we try to measure the radius of an electron, which in experiment after experiment appears to be zero. We calculate the radius using classical tools, but the actual measurement attempts keep indicating this calculation is wrong. That's not a big deal—models are often wrong. The bigger problem is that if the experiments showing no detectable radius are correct, then the charge density of an electron is infinite. It's a division-by-zero issue, and the math blows up on us. Our models of this simplest component of creation are, at the very best, incomplete and, at worst, deeply flawed in ways we don't understand.

In this Holy Week, as we enter the most mysterious part of the church's teaching—the death of the Messiah, the descent of the second person of the Trinity into the grave, and the bursting forth from the tomb—do not worry so much that we don't understand the mechanism. Like our understanding of the nature of the electron, we know only in part, yet knowing in part allows us to peer into the mystery of the whole. We can learn much from our partial knowledge, and we are invited to return again and again to the events of Holy Week, knowing there is still much more there for us to learn.

☙

In what ways is your faith a work in progress? What are you seeking to understand?

Tuesday in Holy Week

What Can We Say About God?

Set your minds on things that are above,
not on things that are on earth.

— Colossians 3:2

One of the most powerful observations theologian Karl Barth made about God and God's action was that everything we say is necessarily limited and incomplete. He compares our efforts to describe God to trying to illustrate the movement of a bird in flight using only words frozen in time and written on a page. There simply isn't any way to adequately explain motion using static ideas. A movie would work better, but even that is a two-dimensional approximation and wouldn't include the experience of the wind, the light, and the rush of the wings pushing against the air.

As human beings, who are created with a beginning and made mortal by our death, we necessarily struggle to think about the eternal divine. We who need to do physical labor and use material to express our creativity can barely comprehend what it would be like to use just our will and potentiality to allow new entities to spring into an autonomous existence. That limitation becomes more evident the more we contemplate the events of Holy Week and the paradoxical implications toward which they lead us.

In theology, we try to understand God's intent in creation and the deeper implications of God's actions in history. But that effort is necessarily limited because we are creatures of God, not God's peers. Just as we struggled to understand our parents' decisions when we were children, we struggle to imagine what God's intentions are, while knowing that we can never experience God's unlimited freedom and creativity in the way we eventually come to understand our parents' actions.

Particularly in Lent, I find that it is only when I can give up my desire to completely understand that I am able to open myself to the unexpected teachings and associations that seem to be part and parcel of the experience of God's actions.

❧

How willing are you to give up the longing that you will ever be able to fully penetrate the mystery of God?

Wednesday in Holy Week

What Is Truth?

Sanctify them in the truth; your word is truth.

— John 17:17

The oddly portentous conversation between Jesus and Pilate at the judgment seat touches directly on one of the most important questions a human being can ask: "What is truth?" (John 18:38). Whether Pilate says it derisively or plaintively depends on how you are reading the account.

Jesus has just replied to Pilate's question about his identity: "You say that I am a king" and "Everyone who is on the side of truth listens to me." If we imagine a hard-boiled, politically savvy Pilate, you can almost hear the snort of derision in his response when he asks, "What is truth?" If we imagine a man caught up in an epic moment of events with cosmic import, you can hear a tone of desperation in his question. While I expect, from what we know of Pilate, that the situation was the former, I find considering the latter to be more profound.

"What is truth?" Jesus doesn't answer Pilate's question. The reason that he doesn't answer is something I have thought about a great deal. There is, of course, the irony, often remarked upon by preachers, that in this moment when Pilate asks the question about the nature of truth, he is sitting in the presence of the fullest expression of God's Truth that we, a part of creation, have ever experienced. Perhaps Jesus doesn't answer because his very presence in that moment is the answer.

Or perhaps the moment of Pilate's question is a theophany—an appearance of God to a mortal being—of the sort that Job experienced when God spoke to him out of the whirlwind. In the book of Job, that righteous man asks again and again to have a chance to confront God and ask, "Why?" When God finally appears to him, God asks Job to first answer questions about the meaning of creation. (I note that God doesn't say Job's answers have to be correct, only that Job offers answers.) But Job doesn't, or can't, answer—the account isn't clear about that. Job, having encountered God, becomes silent.

A rabbi once explained that silence as the expression of Job's realization that it is ultimately impossible for a created mortal being to fully understand the actions of an uncreated, eternal being. It's like trying to explain a three-dimensional object to a two-dimensional being. Or a four-dimensional phenomenon to a three-dimensional being such as ourselves.

There is a school of thought in the study of the philosophy of science, particularly in Karl Popper's work, that starts off by admitting it is impossible in scientific terms to ever know the exact answer to a question. It is possible to get very, very close to the exact answer, but because of the experimentally verified laws of relativity and quantum uncertainty, any answer we provide is going to be inaccurate in absolute terms.

Perhaps that idea too is contained in the silence of Jesus before Pilate, the everyman figure who asks the eternal question of eternity.

∽

Why do you think Jesus keeps silent when questioned?

What do you think is the answer offered by that silence?

Maundy Thursday

What Is the Void?

In the beginning was the Word,
and the Word was with God....
All things came into being through him,
and without him not one thing came into being.
What has come into being in him was life,
and the life was the light of all people.
The light shines in the darkness,
and the darkness did not overcome it.

— John 1:1, 3-5

My strongest and most overwhelming impression of Maundy Thursday is after the service ends—the darkness and the silence of the prayers before the reserved sacrament during the night vigil. Those moments of quiet and prayer have always seemed to me a collective holding of our breath, the long pause before the plunge into the frenzied violence of the events of Good Friday and the shattering sorrow that ends the day.

Over the years, I've reflected how the silence of that experience must reflect the silence of the tomb in which Jesus was to be laid. And I've wondered about the emptiness that he must have experienced in those moments when he was dead.

There's a whole section of theological work, particularly championed in the twentieth century by Urs Van Balthasar, that thought hard about the implications of Jesus' death and the silence of that tomb. This work centered on trying to tease out the meaning of God's abandonment and God's voluntary negation of God's primary characteristics—life and creativity—in that moment. There's much to be learned by thinking that all through.

But as a scientist, I wonder if perhaps all of that effort might be chasing after something that isn't really accurate. As we learn more about the quantum realm of physics, and the implications of the basic equations that govern that counterintuitive space, we are learning that emptiness and vacuum just don't exist. When we peer all the way down to the very smallest scales of the universe, instead of finding a true negative, a place of nothing, what we find instead is a teeming foam of constant improbable creation.

At the smallest scales we speak of something called the quantum foam. The foam is a place where there is constant creation out of nothing, particles springing into existence accompanied by their antimatter counterparts, creating and destroying each other in rapid succession. Such a thing is a direct implication of the uncertainty principle of quantum physics—the rule that it is impossible to know something's energy and time values exactly. This idea is the best explanation to understand why the universe spontaneously sprung into existence out of nothing. And it is into this realm of nothingness that we begin to journey with Jesus in the silent, dark, and empty night of Maundy Thursday.

Jesus' descent into emptiness takes him to the place from which the universe sprang, and from which the new created order he was sent to inaugurate comes as well.

Reflect on the deep truth that emptiness is actually filled with the constant potential of continuous creation. How does this truth change your understanding of the meaning of the absence of life and light, as we know and experience it?

Good Friday

Dark Energy

*The message about the cross is foolishness
to those who are perishing,
but to us who are being saved it is the power of God.*

— 1 Corinthians 1:18

When Einstein first wrote down the equations that are at the heart of his theory of general relativity, he noticed that his equations, as written, indicated that the universe would be unstable. According to his work, the universe would either be expanding or contracting, never found in a constant stable state. So, after some thought, he included a term in the equation—the "cosmological constant"—that had the primary duty of balancing the inherent instability of the structure of space-time.

A few years later, Edwin Hubble published his discovery that the universe was in fact expanding uniformly in all directions. Instead of a stable, eternal universe that people believed had to exist, the universe turned out be moving outward for some reason. Einstein later called his unwillingness to trust his equations and to predict the instability of the universe that Hubble later found the biggest mistake of his life. Einstein then removed the arbitrary constant he had included, and Hubble's work was seen as one of the key validations of his theory.

But decades later, astronomers studying distant supernovae noticed that the rate of the expansion of the universe was not a constant rate as Hubble had seen. With their more precise data and their ability to see much further, they showed that at the edges of the universe, the rate of expansion was accelerating for a reason completely unknown. As people tried to make sense of the data, a few folks returned to the abandoned cosmological constant of Einstein's early work, and pointed out that if it was included, and not used to balance the instability, its presence would allow for the accelerating expansion that was being observed.

Perhaps that term wasn't really Einstein's greatest mistake after all.

At present, theoretical physicists use the term "dark energy" to denote this mysterious energy that is causing the universe to fly outward at all points. We don't know what it is. We cannot see it or measure it. We can only estimate how much of the universe it makes up because we can see the effect it is having on the expansion. And that amount is significant. The best thinking at present is that about 70 percent of the universe is "dark energy." About 25 percent of the universe is made up of something totally different, but with a similar sounding name, the "dark matter." (The "darkness" refers to the fact that the energy and matter in both cases do not emit any light at all that we can detect.) And about 5 percent of the universe is made up of what we can see and detect, ordinary matter and energy.

The present observed structure of the universe cannot be explained unless we include this "dark energy" idea. We don't know what it is, but we know that it is critically important, we would not be here without it, and it is much more common than we ever imagined.

There's a parallel, perhaps mostly poetic but still a parallel, in my mind with this and events of the cross on Good Friday. The unanswerable question, "Why did Jesus have to die on that cross?" has stood as stark challenge to all of us for two thousand years. There is no way at present, perhaps ever, to explain what it means or why it happened. But as Christians we believe that our present existence, our reconciled relationship with God, would not be possible without it. It is critically important: we could not "be" without it, and yet we don't understand it. And more than that, it seems clear that the cross itself signifies a great mystery, whose depths encompass some of the most important questions we ask about our mortality.

The cross is the doorway to these mysteries, just as for scientists the questions about the nature of dark energy seem to indicate there is much more for us to learn than we anticipated. It is my fervent prayer for us as Christians that we will be willing to go to the door that the cross represents with the same tenacity and focus that scientists bring to their study of the created order.

What is the "dark energy" in your faith life?

How does it lead you toward God?

Holy Saturday

The Mystery of Resurrection

For God so loved the world that he gave his only Son,
so that everyone who believes in him may not perish
but may have eternal life.

— john 3:16

What happened in the tomb during the night between Saturday and Easter dawn? No one knows. There's very little we can say about the event scientifically. But something happened. No matter how you want to understand it, as a miracle beyond the ken of scientific knowledge or as a physical phenomenon that we as yet do not understand, clearly something happened. Any examination of the historical evidence leads us to admit that something happened.

As so many people have noted, there's no way to explain the radical shift that occurs in the followers of Jesus, who abandoned him on the morning of Good Friday, cowered in fear in Jerusalem on Holy Saturday, and had some sort of radical life-changing experience on Easter. Whatever happened, it was profound enough that, according to tradition, every single one of apostles was willing to suffer persecution and death because of it. And the people, as eyewitnesses, told about what happened and were willing to follow, not always to their death, but in life-changing ways large and small.

It would be a very lovely thing to be able to explain in detail what happened to Jesus' body; how it was that life returned to it. It would be extraordinary to have firsthand evidence of what the disciples experienced when Jesus met them in the Upper Room or along the road to Emmaus. But we don't have that. And we probably never will. Perhaps that is by God's design.

But I hope as a result of this journey through Lent you are more willing to be comfortable with not understanding something and still accepting its reality. So much of science is in that situation. I've focused on topics of astronomy and physics because that was my early training, but there are mysteries we see but cannot understand in other fields as well. Theology is occasionally described as a discipline that involves faith seeking understanding. The traditional sciences in their own way are disciplines that involve observation seeking understanding. Perhaps the difference between the two is not as great as we often imagine.

Jesus' bodily resurrection challenges us all to question things we don't understand. That willingness to question has led us to many new insights and understandings. But many people react to the unknowns of the resurrection by either trying to explain the resurrection away or by trying to draw a veil around the event and warning people not to enter the sacred precincts. I wonder if, instead of trying to hide the difficulties surrounding the event or trying to resolve them too quickly by denying the reality of the resurrection, we might not better profit by committing ourselves to a journey through the door that the resurrection has opened in our understanding of the world. Perhaps that is the task of the Easter people.

&

The mystery of the resurrection is beyond our human understanding, but its power clearly changed Jesus' disciples. How has it changed you?

Easter Day

The Mystery of Faith

If Christ has not been raised, your faith is futile
and you are still in your sins.
Then those also who have died in Christ have perished.
If for this life only we have hoped in Christ,
we are of all people most to be pitied.
But in fact Christ has been raised from the dead,
the first fruits of those who have died.

— 1 Corinthians 15:17-20

I suppose our scientific worldview and our religious faith find the most fundamental conflict in the question of Jesus' bodily resurrection. The stories of creation have been historically understood as stories, not as scientific arguments, and the apparent conflict between the two worldviews is relatively easy to resolve. But when we assert the literal understanding of the bodily resurrection—the miracle of the undoing of death—we can find no simple path to resolution. Either Jesus rose from the dead or he didn't. As Saint Paul writes to the Corinthians, this was not understood as a metaphor. It was understood to be literally true.

What are we to make of such a claim, given our modern, scientific worldview? We might argue it away by saying it was just a sense that people had of Jesus' presence among them even after his horrible death. Certainly some have made this argument. We might even want to argue that the question of the bodily resurrection isn't that important and at least one of the gospels (Mark's) doesn't explicitly include it.

But Paul's writing insists that it is true. And if it were not true, then all the people who have followed Jesus, because he was explicitly identified as the Messiah, because of his resurrection (not resuscitation), must be deeply wrong. Paul argues that it is in the literal and bodily resurrection that all of our hopes as Christian people are centered.

So, can it be true? Doesn't science say it is impossible? Isn't entropy, i.e., randomness and disorder, always increased? Once decay begins, how can it be reversed?

Here's the thing. Science is very good at describing how repeatable events happen. Science has nothing to say about the miraculous, except that it is not predictable or explainable by using the tools of the scientific method. But that doesn't mean it didn't happen. It means rather that such a question is unanswerable by the scientific method.

As powerful as the scientific method is, and even with all the wonders we have achieved by its use, it is still not a complete description of the universe. As we have discussed in this booklet, there are things that are true that cannot be logically proven to be true. Such is the case with the miraculous and particularly with the central event of the Christian faith, the resurrection.

As many have pointed out, the proof of the resurrection is not found in a scientific understanding of what happened. It is found in the lives of the men and women who, having experienced it, were willing to die to proclaim its truth to those who had not seen it.

If you are asked to prove the truth of the resurrection, the only argument you will be able to make is that of the life you are leading.

Alleluia! Christ is risen.
The Lord is risen indeed. Alleluia.

About the Author

W. Nicholas Knisely was ordained the thirteenth bishop of the Episcopal Diocese of Rhode Island in November 2012.

He holds degrees in physics and astronomy from Franklin and Marshall College in Lancaster, Pennsylvania, and the University of Delaware and a master of divinity degree from the Berkeley Divinity School at Yale in New Haven, Connecticut. Prior to his ordination as bishop, he served as a priest in Delaware, Western and Eastern Pennsylvania, and as Dean of the Cathedral in Phoenix, Arizona.

Knisely was the first chair of The Episcopal Church's Standing Commission on Communications and has served on various national and international bodies in that field. He maintains a personal blog called "Entangled States" and is a member of the Episcopal Network for Science, Technology, & Faith. He and his wife Karen have been married for thirty years and have an adult daughter.